It's Not Gunna Be an Addiction

The Adolescent Journals
of Amy Caruso
(1989–2009)

Amelia F. W. (Amy) Caruso
Edited by Melissa M. Weiksnar

Amelibro Press

Published by Amelibro Press LLC
P.O. Box 251
Carlisle, MA 01741

www.amelibro.com

www.itsnotgunnabeanaddiction.com

Library of Congress Control Number: 2014951987
ISBN: 978-0-9854787-3-5

Printed in the United States of America
The Troy Book Makers • www.thetroybookmakers.com

Cover photo by Lifetouch

Book design by Laurel Lloyd

To Amy

and to everyone else who has been touched by addiction

It's not gunna be an addiction but at least I can say I did it w/out lying. Also, now I won't be so obsessed w/drugs b/c I've tried em, so I know how they r now.

—*summer before sophomore year of high school*

Contents

A Note to Readers

Amy Caruso was the youngest of my three children. She was a smart, feisty, and social child who enjoyed so much life has to offer, but she had a rough time in high school. She had depression, anxiety, and struggles with her self esteem, which she could hide with her friendliness and cheerful manner. In ninth grade she began self-medicating with cutting, and was prescribed an antidepressant. She started using caffeine pills, and then sleeping pills to compensate. After many months of thinking and writing about it, she began smoking marijuana. By the time she was a sophomore she was using cocaine, and during her junior year, I found the prescription painkiller Vicodin in her purse. She first tried heroin at seventeen, used some OxyContin in college, and admitted a few months into her junior year of nursing college that she was addicted to heroin and wanted to go to treatment. Less than six weeks later, she died from an overdose at the treatment facility, weeks shy of her twenty-first birthday.

Amy left the world an incredible gift: the journals she kept from middle school through her weeks in her addiction rehabilitation program (rehab). I shared her rehab journals in *Heroin's Puppet -Amy (and her disease)*. That book was mainly for parents, educators, and clinicians. This book is for young people who want to read about someone going from innocent little girl to a young woman who lost her life to addiction.

These journals are a difficult read. At times Amy felt she didn't have anyone who understood her. We can only imagine how her life may have turned out differently if she hadn't been so afraid to talk about her pain instead of just write. Or if a she had been able to read a book like this one.

You might ask if I've violated her privacy by publishing the journals. I've wrestled with that question a lot, and found my answer in the "Bucket List" she wrote during treatment (see page 184), which included:

- Change someone's life for the better
- Make a completely unique contribution to the world
- Make a difference
- Touch someone's heart

These entries give me the faith that sharing her journals enables Amy to fulfill her bucket list in a way she can no longer do in person—and she was always making lists and crossing off what she did. So sharing Amy's journals is not only her gift to you: it is also a gift to her.

Melissa Weiksnar
September 2013

About Amy's Journals

Amy wrote the majority of her adolescent journals by hand. (She probably wrote more on her computers, but we have not been able access those entries.) After she died, I transcribed the handwritten entries, preserving her original spelling, grammar, and punctuation for authenticity. To avoid distraction, I have not used [sic] after errors. Where feasible, her formatting (line spacing, indents, justifications, etc.) was preserved. The colors in the eBook edition are very similar to the actual ink she used unless the color would be too difficult to read, in which case it was changed to black.

Many of Amy's abbreviations and slang words will be familiar. To help international readers and because language changes over time, the full English word is given in double brackets [[like this]] the first time the term is used, except where Amy dropped the final "g" (e.g., goin rather than going).

Except for public figures and some family members, I have changed the names of all people (and, in some cases, identifying details) and most places. The same pseudonyms from *Heroin's Puppet* are used in this book.

To protect the privacy of Amy's friends, I've omitted some details, including those about some sexual experiences. Amy occasionally used homosexual slurs until she was sixteen. I did not strike those references, even though she knew they were unacceptable in our home.

Omissions for privacy, confidentiality, or brevity are noted by the brackets [...], which should not be confused with the places where Amy ended a thought with multiple periods. Substitutions are also in single brackets [like this]. My commentary appears under a dotted line in italics.

I've shared my daughter's journals as a mother. My training is in economics, engineering, and business, and I have no professional education in psychology or substance abuse treatment. I am providing neither advice nor recommendations, but I have included a little bit about resources at the end of the book.

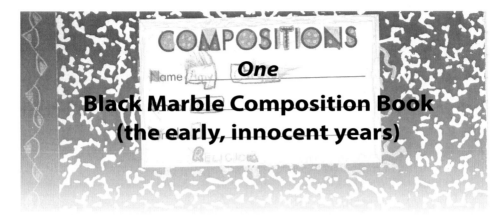

One

Black Marble Composition Book
(the early, innocent years)

December 25, 1995[1]
Got Dolly maker for Christmas. Got lots of good toys. Went to Grandma and Grandpas house had a fun time.

January 1, 1996
Did a word puzzle with mom. [...]

May 18, 1997[2]
[...]Rode bikes with [my friend]. Planted my seedlings with Mom. Did ape imitations. Love Opal Fruits.

June 1999 note of apology to the school librarian[3]:
I'm sorry for talking when the lights were out [in the library]. I'm not trying to make excuses but I do think that some other people (not mentioning names) were somewhat causing me to get into trouble. Talking is one of my main hobbies and I sometimes just talk without thinking. I apologize completely for talking and I will try not to talk when the lights are off again.

Fall 1999[4]
My Parents
pays for my tuition
heal me when I'm sick
talk to me when I feel lonely/something happens

---

1. Amy is in the first grade, almost 7.
2. Amy is almost 8½, living in England.
3. It is the end of fourth grade. Amy is almost 10½, back in the U.S.A.
4. Amy is in the fifth grade and 10½.

give me all my needs
never stop loving me
tell me what is right + wrong
encourage me all the time
went through labor

I think the sweetest sound in the world is my sisters voice when she sees me
and says 'Hello Pumpkin Face' and hugs me and Gill Shaham playing the
violin. My mom playing cello and my dad singing.

Qualities I admire
no lieing a lot
someone who won't tell my darkest secrets
laughs when me or my sister tell jokes.
who gets my sick jokes.
trusts me
cares if I get hurt
doesn't talk behind my back
likes my hobbies
doesn't brag a lot
doesn't diss boys.
has good taste
brave
adventures
isn't scared of big kids.

11/8/99
Gifts from God
my sister
my brother
me
my freinds and family
not retarded (nothing wrong)
not in a wheelchair
animals
not yet very bad deaseize

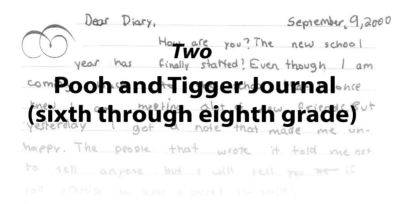

September, 9, 2000[1]

Dear Diary

How are you? The new school year has finally started! Even though I am coming back to the school that I once knew, I am meeting a lot of new friends. But yesterday I got a note that made me unhappy. The people that wrote it told me not to tell anyone but I will tell you if you promise to keep a secret. It said:

YO, AMY!
HAVE YOU FORGOTTEN YOUR
<u>OLD</u> FRIEND?
SIGNED, YOUR 3 OLD BEST FRIENDS
MEREDITH AACHEN, ALICE BAALBEK, OLIVIA CABAN

I am confused dear diary. I never thought they were my <u>best</u> friends. Today is Mommy and Daddys Anniversary. I am writing them a card. Dad just gave mom a gardening set since she misplaced her old one. Mom is giving him some mums tomorrow. I saw my friend Agnes Dacca at church today. She and her family just moved here and they are <u>really</u> nice. Gotta [[Have to]] go do my homework. – AMY

11/26/00 – I don't like Ophelia anymore. Ophelia is a bitch.

October 17

Dear Diary,

The school year has been very challenging so far. I really like this 1 boy though. His name is Byron Faenza. He is really nice and really hot. Today i gave him a list of girls so he can say if he likes me or not. I want him as a boyfriend

_____

1. Amy is in the sixth grade, 11½.

soooo [[so]] bad but my friend Angeline Gabes (I hate her) would kill me! She 'went out' with him for 2 days. Byron is really hot and my goal is to go out with him by the end of the year. I'm gonna [[going to]] write in a little prayer:

> "Dear God, may [my two aunts] get better, may I do well in school, and dear Lord will you help me go out with ~~Byron~~ Isaiah by the end of the year and dance with him by the next dance. Thank-you! –Amy"

Please make my wish come true!
–Amy

October 18

Dear Diary,

Today was fun, but hectic! I think my prayer is working! Byron asked Evangeline if I liked him! That means he wanted to go out with me! Only problem is, she said I liked him but don't want to go out with him. Byron is soooo hot! And nice!

Tuesday, Nov. 9

Dear Diary,

Byron is my friend now and he is going out with my BFF [[best friend forever]] Evangeline Iasi. I am actually going out with somebody named Rupert Jabalpur. I really like him.
–Amy

Nov. 16

Dear Diary,

Rupert dumped me after 1 week 1 day ☹. He is now going out with my friend Jocelyn. This kid Noah Labuan likes me and I am going to the Formal dance (called the Snow Ball Dance) with him. Speaking of the formal, the couples are on the next page. But first, here are the people I like:

Lucian Merida (nice)
Rupert Jabalpur (still)
Noah Labuan (nice)
Byron Faenza (my BFF, nice)
Pedro Naas (hot)
Lawrence Oakham (hot + funny)

Amy made a list of twenty-one Snow Ball Couples

Dear Diary-

I have so much to say. [...]Jocelyn dumped Rupert! They r [[are]] friends now. He is still going to the dance with her and he is gonna ask her, and his new crush Monica to dance at Friday night live (FNL). [...] Byron is a little annoying. He calls me every night and I think he likes me. Evangeline is gonna dump him right after the s.b.[...] I am gonna see how the week goes with guys and I will make a new list at the end of the week. Right now the only person I sorta [[sort of]] like like, is:
RUPERT JABALPUR

Please help him to like me more!
–Amy ☺

Dear Diary,

GUESS WHAT?! Rupert asked me out again! I said yes! I am really happy but he says he likes someone else too (Thelma). I like:
Rupert Jabalpur – ~~80%~~ 100%
~~Stuart Tablas = 10%~~
~~Isiaih Habana --- 10%~~
He likes me 80% and <u>Thelma</u> 20%. Anyway, I gtg [[got to go]] to b-ball [[basketball]] practice – bye.

Dear Diary –

Today was a good and bad day. Well, the bad thing first. Well, I had this tattoo on my belly that said "I ♥ RUPERT J" and my mom saw it! She was pretty darn pissed! Now the good news. I hug danced with RUPERT!!! It was soooo cool! I had my head on his shoulder! I looooved it!!! [...]

By the way – I like:
Rupert - 100%

Jan 14, 01[2]

Dear Diary –

Rupert + me have been going out for 6 weeks. WOW! He is so shallow, he was gonna dump me for someone more popular – Maxine. I really like him though. Guess what? Byron AND Noah like me!!! Byron has seriously asked me out like 10x and he told me to dump Rupert for him!! [My aunt] died though ☹. Oh, here are the people i like (almost forgot):

> Rupert – (mixed feelings)
> Lucian – (the teeniest %)

I am really upset that he was gonna dump me but i still really like him. gtg. Bye-bye.

Amy Caruso

Dear Diary,

Hi! I have had a very, very intresting few weeks. I <u>love</u> Cruel Intentions (the movie). I am <u>still</u> going out with Rupert but all my friends are making me dump him. I like other people but I like him too and I'm really confused and….. Oh well i will just tell you my crushes (the chemicals)

> ♥ Isaiah Habana ♥
> ♥ Gary Ubange ♥

Byron loves my guts + everybody wants me to go out with him. I am getting a haircut tomorrow. I'm really upset cuz' [[because]] my grades are not great and no one's really there to help me. Oh well. There's a new kid named Monty. He's cute. Omg [[Oh my god]], that's gross I gtg. (bedtime). see ya [[you]]!

–Amy ☺
p.s. I don't like Byron anymore @ [[at]] all so i changed the prayer.

Hi Diary–
I ♥ Gary
I dumped Rupert + i feel great! Gary asked me out I ♥ gary I ♥ gary I ♥ gary I LOVE HIM . He's the hottest guy on school campus. He loves me; i love him…. I hope we never break up. i will stick in some pics [[pictures]] of Mr. Sexy when i have more time. I ♥ gary   I ♥ gary
Amy

---

2. Amy is in the sixth grade, almost 12.

P.S. Evangeline ♥ BYRON
I ♥ gary   I wanna [[want to]]
            kiss him!!
            (lips)
            I ♥ gary

Dear Diary,

Hi! I am wicked obsessed w/ [[with]] Gary. He is popular, nice, funny, HOT, cool. … I LUV [[LOVE]] HIM! I made a tattoo on my ankle for him: [I ♥ Ubange] Which is totally true. The annoying thing is, i was in his group (Olympics) for 3 weeks when we weren't going out and now i am in NONE of his classes and Evangeline is in 2 of them. I hate the way she ALWAYS flirts with him. Well, just pray that I'll be in his Outdoor ed. group. Here's a prayer, PLEASE MAKE IT COME TRUE and i will not pester my mom for a LONG time + no gmby [[Game Boy (handheld electronic device)]] race car game:

> Dear God,
> I love you. I love gary.
> I just wanna say this prayer
> cause' i finally know what
> true love is. I would love
> it if you could make
> gary NEVER dump me and
> if we ever break up it
> will be my choice (which'll never happen)
> + please make us kiss lips (soon)
> AND French (eventually).
> and could we go to either
> each others house or
> the movies by the end

of 2 months? Call each other every day I want us to be EXACTLY like Elinor + Lawrence + Never ever ever ….. (x = infinity) break up. Please make Daddy's back get better, mom's depression better + my wish come true. Thank you! Luv, Amy

Like it????? I haven't talked to Gary @ all today but i will definetly call him tomorrow. I saw Josie + The Pussycats today. It ROCKED! Me, Agnes Dacca + Evangeline are making a band. Look:

Possible Nicknames	Possible band names
Sugar	Faith
Spice	Sugar Babes
Zest	Bliss
A-anxious	
L - l	
s - s	
sweet	

G2G2 [[got to go to]] Sleep. see ya.

~ Amy Caruso

6-18

Dear Diary,

Today a 7th grader from the the next town over hung himself. I didn't know him but its a huge shock. My mom is having <u>HUGE</u> mood swings like today she took away the portable phone [...] but today she offered to take me to ice-cream + bonded w/ me. [...] School is <u>AWESOME</u>. At least the social part (hehehe). Me and Evangeline got invited into the 'popular' group ☺. She is getting closer to them + more far apart from me so that's the bad part. Gary and i are still going out but all the dances are over ☹. Rosemary is having a b-day [[birthday]] party on the 23rd. Gary and i are going! 35 PEEPS [[people]] R GOIN!!! Uh-oh. Pubirty is starting. My boobs are growin, getting a little hair, i am shaving. And..... well..... i think my hormones are really buzzing because..... i really want to make out or do stuff w/ gary. Hopefully it is normal. Gary and I don't talk <u>AS MUCH</u> as b4 [[before]] but oh well.

GARY is SEXY

I ♥ gary

Lucian likes me!
BFF's = Evangeline + Hazel.
g2g, bed. Bye!

–Amy

7-2

Hi! Rosemary's party was great! Gary kissed me on the cheek + hand (dare). He's kissed me on the lips ONCE. We joke around A LOT which is fun. God, I am asking so much but please listen to this prayer:

I♥SPORTS

Dear God. I promise to be Catholic 4eva [[forever]]. I Love you Jesus. I need you do to a couple things tho [[though]]: please make gary + i neva [[never]] eva [[ever]] break up, please please please make us make out in 7th grade, also same hmrm [[homeroom]], be loyal to me + us go on a date or double date. Please + Thank you for everythin! -Amy

I am going to softball + b-ball camp w/ Evangeline next week. It is gonna RULE! [...] g2g to bed, please work on the prayers?

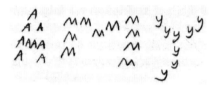

Dear Diary,

I am going to a sleepaway camp really soon. (4 days). I am soooo exited! The only downside is, none of my friends go there!!! I will hav [[have]] to make new ones. i am nervous but also exited. Gary is away till 2morrow [[tomorrow]]. EVANGELINE IS MOVING
☹ ☹ ☹ ☹ ☹ ☹ ☹ ☹ ☹

[…] How am i gonna live??? OK, well i g2g (lunch). C ya [[see you]]

~ Amy

Nov 10th
2002

Dear Diary,

Hey ~ Sorry I haven't written in so long, i just found you! Anyways let me tell you a little about myself. I'm 13½ years old and my birthday is Jan. 20th. I'm in the 8th grade and lovin it. Throughout my life I've had 3 boyfriends. I'll tell you about them. First: Rupert Jabalpur. He was my first boyfriend ever. Wicked sweet. Kinda [[kind of]] cute. […] Making me horny just thinking about it. Ok I really need to stop now because he'd never go out w/ me again – I'm as flat as a snow board! I have no boobs! It's seriously not fair b/c [[because]] guys check out and judge by boobs all the time but when girls go to do that w/ guys all there is is cock and you can barely see them. Okay now something that will turn me off.... Isaiah Habana. Ugh! Ugliest kid I've ever seen I guess I just went out w/ him because he lives really close and I thought we could maybe have a kind of good relationship. I was wrong. I dumped him in like 2 months. Ok now I really need to talk about Gary. He was an amazing boyf [[boyfriend]]. We have so much in common. I feel like I know exactly what his life is like because that's how I'm living too. We've gone out alltogether on and off for about 10 months. During all of 6th and most of 7th grade we were all shy around each otther but now it's like we are <u>such</u> good friends. Honestly, I still have some sexual feelings for him. We flirt a lot but no matter what, he always seems to like someone else. I think that's partly my fault though because I dumped him at the beginning of this year. Worst mistake ever. I can't put in words how much I still like him. I'll talk more about him later. Right now I wanna talk about prudeness. That is a huge problem here in Town. All the people are like OMG THEY KISSED! I dont understand why though. I've made out w/ 3 guys and grinded w/ one. OMG I totally forgot about my camp boyf! I cheated on Gary w/ him shhh but then I dumped him. We went so fast though I'm talking make-out and grinding in 3 days! I was like hell yeah! Anyways if I had a BF right now I'd go all out – make out, up his shirt (not mine cuz [[because]] I have no boobs), Down the pants, hand job, blow job! But I dont wanna have sex till HS [[High School]]. Any ways I'm tired, I better sleep. WTYL! [[write to you later]]

   ~ Amy

[It's] the day after thanksgiving, the 29th. [...] Okay well lemme [[let me]] go over a quick summary of my social life. For friends ~ I am in the "popular" group now. Hilary Abaco was one of my best friends but now I'm probly [[probably]] closest with Maeve. As far as my marital status ~ I'm single! I kind of like this kid from the next town over, Woodrow Ceara, but I've never even met him before, just seen him in a videotape of Isaac's Bar-mitzvah. He's sleeping over Isaac's tonight and since I live so close to the Dearborn's, I might get to go see him ☺! Vivian lives close, and she likes Elvin who is also sleeping over Isaac's so we might go to a movie or something. WISH ME LUCK!

  ~ Amy Caruso

[undated]
Dear Diary,

Good morning! I just woke up, it's like 10am. Today me and my mom are going shopping for basketball stuff. You wanna know something weird? Well this weekend I saw the movie 'the ring' with Hilary and Gary. Anyways it was the freakiest movie I've ever seen! So damn scary. It's about a girl and she puts out a video tape and when you watch this tape, you have 7 days until you die. It's sooo [[so]] scary w/ a lot of popouts. Anyways when I was babysitting (the night after) [missing][...]

[undated]
Dear Diary ~

OMG I'm so incredibly mad! Here's my story. Okay well Hilary basically runs Garys life. She tells him what to do, who to like, how to "fit in" etc. He knows it too! Okay well she made him wear this really gay outfit so I was like "Gary don't let her tell you what to do" and he told Hilary! EVERYONE hates Hilary, ME, MAEVE, VIVIAN, OPHELIA, CLARICE and like 50 more ppl [[people]] are in an 'I Hate Hilary' club. Gary used to be until he said that. Anyways – i haven't been talking to him and Rosemary told him that I cheated on him! Bitch! IDK [[I Don't Know]] what to do! I really don't want my rep. [[reputation]] ruined even though its my fault. gotta get some z's [[sleep]] cya [[see you]].
          ~Amy

June 9th, 2003
Dear Diary,

OMG I have sooo much to tell you. I'm over Gary. Over the 5 months I've been gone, I've gone out with Noah, Horacio, and Niko. First of all Horacio. I wrote a 2 page journal entry on how much i loved him, i'll paste it in lata [[later]], but anyways people took my diary, and overnight the whole school had read it.

....

The next entry is the one Amy mentions above as having been stolen and read by her classmates.

                                                                    3/21/03

Dear Journal,

Hello, my name is Amy. This is a continuation from my old journal, which I accidentally misplaced. Anyways, have been wanting to write in a diary for the longest time but I haven't been able to find a good one. Well, mainly what I've been wanting to get out is about my boyfriend, Horacio. It all started out in early January, that's when I was in Horacio's LA [[Language Arts]] team. The sparks were there, but I didn't think they were big. Later that month I realized that this was the kind of guy I wanted to be with. I admitted my crush for him first to my friend Maeve. Unfortunately, the next day our seats in LA got changed. Anyways, there was a dance just before Feb. vacation and he asked me to dance. Even though he had to leave early, it was still an amazing night because I found out he liked me too. When the vacation was over, we experienced the first week knowing each other liked the other one. It was really awkward, but we got by. In the next few weeks we started talking on the phone and Horacio kept telling everybody he was gonna ask me out. Anyways he kept not doing it when he said he was, so I was kind of losing hope. Then, I skipped 3rd row Celts tickets to go to a dance. It was 9:33, the end of the dance, and I was upset that Horacio still hadn't asked me out. Little did I know that he was waiting till this time to do it since 33 is my lucky number. [...]

....

Most students from Amy's middle school went on to Regional Public High School, the local public high school. But Amy's father and I felt she would fare better in a smaller school. We wanted her to attend the all-girls Catholic school where I taught. The letter that follows expresses Amy's position. After a lot of back and forth, Amy and Lily agreed to attend the Catholic school together.

Summer 2003 letter re: high school decision [3]

Hey Mom and Dad,
I am writing to talk to you about the BVMP [[Blessed Virgin Mary Preparatory]] decision. I know you really want me to go there, but I have soooo many reasons why I know it would be better for me to go to RPHS [[Regional Public High School]]. Over the years I have changed schools about 6 times. For once in my life I thought that I would actually be able to stay set where I am right now and actually go into high school with my friends…I am completely sick of all the new friends I have had to make, and lose. For once I am becoming very very very close to a lot of kids at my middle school, and now you are trying to take that away from me. You say that you will let me stay very close to my friends, but that's also what you said

---

3. Amy is 14½.

when I left for fifth grade and I ended up staying close with Evangeline, and that was because she lived less than half a mile away so I could easily bike to her house. (With people like Lily, I can't do that because they live much farther away.) Still my friend and I only saw each other about 3 times in the full year. I tried an all girls environment in fifth grade and it doesn't work for me. My first choice in school was RPHS, even over boarding school. While I am writing this letter, I'm crying, because I cannot imagine having to change schools again, and again attend an all girls' school. On my visiting day there, the teachers were ok, but I found on my half day at RPHS, the teachers were a lot stronger in what they taught, and they really got the message across to me. At BVMP, I was practically falling asleep during each of the classes, and I didn't learn anything new. Also at BVMP, all I heard was gossip among the students, during classes, recess, and lunch, even church. Now I do know that I gossip a bit, I'll admit to that, but in one 45 minutes lunch period, I probably heard more gossip than I heard in 1 month at my school. With all girls, that is basically all there is to do, and I can't stand it. Fifth grade was like that and the only thing that kept me sane was my friend. Also I do not want to go to a school that my own mother teaches at. When Mom taught religious education for my grade, I completely misbehaved because it felt like I was at home, so I felt like I could do whatever I wanted. I don't want to have to go through four years of high school like this. BVMP doesn't have Latin or Orchestra, and RPHS has both of those plus about 832,647,153 different groups and clubs that BVMP doesn't have. Also, I was kind of looking forward to going to BVMP with Olivia […] but now that she's probably not going to BVMP, my opinion has been greatly affected, and even if she were going, it would still be very very difficult. I am just sooooo upset that you already made my high school decision already… and I'm not saying I never want to go to BVMP, it's just that I'm not ready to go this year and I'm begging you to PLEASE reconsider and respect my input, because I know that I would try really hard at RPHS and I honestly think it is the best decision. If I thought BVMP was the right decision, the thing about my friends wouldn't bother me that much, but I know it is not the right decision. Please reconsider because I am miserable):):):

~Love, Amy
P.S. I have many more reasons but I think the letter is long enough as it is.

Three
Purple Suede Journal
(ninth grade)

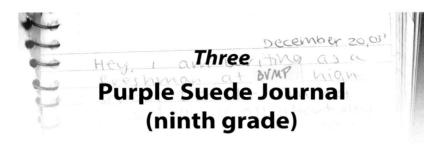

December 20, 03[1]

Hey, I am writing as a freshman at BVMP high school. I'm 14. I'm not gonna tell u [[you]] all about my background b/c i've done that so much in all my other diaries but ya [[yes]] dude, i'm in so much trouble. i was just on the phone w/ my friend lily + her boyf after my phone ~~time~~ curfew and my dad found out + i lied about it and then he found out i was lying. Shit i'm so fucked. I mite [[might]] get my cell taken away. Anyways idk i'm under so much fuckin pressure right now, like idk my parents used to have rules, and then they let loose a little, but now i do really bad in school and now i can't go on trips to FLA [[Florida]]. but idk, i seriously cannot focus on my homework. like i sit down for an hour tryin to do it and i can't. It's like I know I need more rules, but when i get more rules I hate it and i just feel like breaking them more. thats another thing, like i know what i need but i don't want what i need. I deffinately need a shrink but theres no way i can do that because i feel like i'm always right and i hate when ppl analyze me. I really wanna start up w/ drugs, like i tell every1 [[everyone]] i do drugs and they believe me b/c i'm such a trouble maker @ school (i have the detention record!). I'm friggen notorious at BVMP. It's awesome. Anyways ya I never wanna smoke cigarettes but i sooo wanna do weed [[marijuana]] and sum hallucinagens mite b [[be]] good 2. Dude, now u c what I mean? Like last year I would have never even considered drugs but now I would like kill sum1 [[someone]] for them. Anyways I'm afraid 2 leave my room b/c i'm afraid my dads gonna yell @ me for the cell phone thing and i'm gonna have to lie more. Dude, my advice is to never lie. I have lied to every single person I've ever talked to. It's like 1ce [once] you lie and get away w/ it once

---

1. Amy is almost 15.

you can't stop. I think I'm a pathological liar. And also I seriously like hurt myself for attention sumtimes. Like so ppl will b like 'omg Amy u poor thing!'. Idk, i'm getting betta [[better]] w/ that tho. Dude there's so many fucken ppl that have had sex in my school already i'm gonna make a list of all the ppl that aren't virgins. [...] and...ya i think thats it. (List of ppl who do drugs: [...] and not sure who else). But its like WOW! I never thought so many ppl would have done it. Dude, I was thinking more about myself. What if I've been bullshitting myself? What if I just feel bad for myself so I'm making up all these problems? I can't deal w/ it though, whether my problems are real or fake. Dude my pen's like smoking cuz i'm writing so fast. I NEED FUCKIN PROZAC. I swear I'm depressed inside! Dude I also owe my parents a shitload of $ to pay em' back for my computer and shit. It's like I have so much shit that I need to take care of but I always think 'Oh, i'll do it later' and then i never do. I need a fucken psychiatrist. U know what else though? I wanna be a psychiatrist so the thought of going to one feels pointless. And it's crazy like you would never expect all these problems from me. I'm such a happy person. I have to keep my emotions inside because if I tell anyone they will think i'm crazy. Who knows? Maybe I am crazy. But I will never tell anyone. It's really sad because I want to have a future. I don't wanna grow up and live on the streets. I want to go to Duke. I wanna have a good life when I'm older. I find tho that when I think about my future I want to totally change and start over, but then when it comes to the moments when I could make things better I don't want to. I think I'm too concerned about bein popular tho. Like I friggen stay online like 24-7 just so Elyssa will IM [[Instant Message]] me. Like I guess cuz I was cool (popular) in my Town it's weird to be kind of weird (a loser) at BVMP. Whatever though I think I'm gonna go now, and I'm probly goin over Helmut's house 2mrw [[tomorrow]] w/ Rosanne Ubangi and Clinton but I'll write in you lata. Thanks for letting me steam to you.

♥ Amy

December 21

Heyhey!

What's up? Today I went to the mall with my friend Lily Jackson. Dude idk about her b/c last year i was like sooo much cooler than her but it's like this year @ our new school she is tryin hella [[really]] hard to be more popular. It pisses me off. And like she [...] tries so hard to look good. Whatever I am trying to get her to leave next year. She is. It'll be weird though b/c even though i hate her, she's my best friend too. Like we have so many inside jokes and like she's totally my security friend @ BVMP. I totally miss Maeve tho. She was my BFF last year. It was so different w/ her. I loved our friendship soo [[so]] much. Oh well, it is over now that I'm @ BVMP. Now back to me being a liar (we talked a lil [[little]] about this yesterday). Like I'm so serious. I lie about everything. I can't help it. I always tell myself I'll stop but then I don't. Like when stuff comes up that I can't get out of, I'll lie about it. I don't even know. Anyways @ the mall there was this guy @ Dunkin' Donuts and he said 2 tell Lily that she was wearing a hott shirt and that she was hott. I'm still in total shock. Like she was wearing like the whoriest shirt I've ever seen!!! A v-neck halter top!!! It's crazy like last year nobody in the whole school thought she was pretty at all and now i guess she is. But i guarentee u if she came out w/ no make up, no special hair do, no tight shirts, she'd look so fucking ugly. Idk what I'm saying I mean I guess part of it is jealosy [[jealousy]], but still… and it really pisses me off b/c she always bullshits and she just happens to never have any clean shirts that aren't v-necks but that's the only reason she wears them and she claims Maeve's clothes were much worse. Whatever. Maeve wouldn't be caught dead in a shirt like that. Aright [[All right]] well I'm gunna [[going to]] go 2 sleep rite now, its 1:38 and I gotta go to 9 am church 2mrw. Wish me luck wakin up!

    ~Amy ♥

December 22

Yo yo yo,

OK well this has been a fucken eventful night. I went to the mall w/ Audrey + Lily J. Audrey is fucken hilarious. She goes up to random guys and asks them for their #'s. We musta [[must have]] gotten @ least #10 diff. number's. Dude tho, we saw some of her old friends in the food court and they had weed so later Audrey called them and we were about to go out and smoke but then I chickened out (cuz i've never fucken done it – i'm all talk) and i just waited in weather vane w/ Lily. The one thing Lily doesn't know is that Audrey brought back some grass and gave it to me. Theres only like 3 little kernels of it but Audrey says thats enough to smoke it out of a soda can or something. I wanna try it so bad but idk, i mean the #1 person I'd wanna tell about it is Lily J., but she would never talk to me again if she found out i did that. I'm still pondering it. Earlier I touched it, and my hands still stink from the smell. [...] Ugh i'm under so much stress – i have no fucken idea what to get my brother for Christmas. I have no money ☹ [...] My life has so many dilemmas … sometimes i just wanna get away but i keep strong, putting 1 foot ahead of another until i'm there. Every day is a milestone. Going to bed. TTYL [Talk To You Later].

    ~Amy ♥

YO,   December 23,2003
I didn't have that much of an eventful day today. I went to my middle school to visit my old teachers. Then I went to the mall then I came home, went online and watched tv till now (2:45 in the morning). So it's actually Christmas Eve right now – yay! Since i don't have that much news to tell you i'll talk about BVMP. At BVMP i'm like the class troublemaker. I am there to piss people off and get in trouble. I break all the rules, and sometimes I find myself doing stuff on purpose to get yelled @ cuz everyone thinks its funny and I have a reputation to uphold. I hold the record for detentions. Niko IM'd me tonight. I miss him. Niko was the boy I cheated on Horacio with and went out with for about 3 months (end of 8th grade till mid summer). He lives over an hour away so I only saw him 2ce [[twice]] (we met up secretly @ red sox games). He was such an amazing boyfriend though. We talked for 4 hours a day on the phone and when we couldn't talk on the phone, we text messaged each other. He made me feel good, when I felt like shit. When even my closest friends weren't there for me, Niko was. I don't remember how it ended but i do remember that no words can describe how much that kid meant to me. Oh well ☹ I think I have a sleeping problem. I seriously stayed up the entire night last wednesday and the next day I stayed up till midnight even tho i had school that day! Thats 43 hours of nonstop awakeness plus school! Haha. Oh well. Audrey called tonight. She wants me to meet up w/ her and some druggies we met at the mall tomorrow. I donno [[don't know]] if i should but i don't have anyone really to talk me out of it. Oh yeah Rosanne Ubangi's bringin me prozac when we get back to school yay! It'll make me happy! Audrey says if ur [[you are]] not depressed it makes u wicked annoyin tho too bad LOL [[Laughing Out Loud]]. I'm takin it rite b4 school start's – piss off all the teachers ☺ ttyl!
  ♥ Amy

                                                            Christmas Eve
Hey, Today was kinda eventful i guess. I woke up and had my dad bring me dunkin donuts. Then I went to church and learned how to serve again because I forgot. Then Audrey called and she wanted to see if I wanted to smoke weed w/ her and her friends today. I kinda wish that I told her the truth; that i've never done drugs but idk i just lied. Oh well i can't take it back now right? K [[okay]] well then i came home and went online and started packing for my grandparents' b/c i leave for there tomorrow. Then @ 11 we went off to midnight mass and I was an altar server there. There was this old guy there who kept winking @ me – sketchy huh? Now its like

1:45 AM on Christmas. I'm soooo excited. Actually I'm not. That was a lie. I am probably the least excited i have ever been about Christmas. I don't know it's just like i can't feel the spirit. All the time now it feels like theres a wall around me taking away from all my senses. I feel like just a blob. And I'm also not excited because i don't think my parents got me anything from my list. I guess it's my fault because my grades are so bad. They just put my presents under the tree—i can't wait till i see them! I'll tell you what i got in the morning! TTYL!

    ~Amy ♥

Yo,   Dec. 25, 03

Today was Christmas. Like I expected it was not very good. OK so I don't expect that much for Christmas but I have some expectations. From my parents I got a book on snowflakes and this Burts beeswax kit ($9) and a Starbucks giftcard. They also got a combined gift for the 3 kids. A dryer. A fucking dryer. I made up a Christmas list like 2 months ago and you wanna know something? I didn't get 1 thing from that list. Oh well. Right now I'm in at our condo [[family condominium about two hours from home]] … we're on our way to my grandparents' but it's snowing there so we have to spend the night here. New Years is comin up. I hella wanna go party but Lily J. is gone till Jan. 6th so I can't chill w/ her but I'm scared if I chill w/ Audrey she's gunna wanna smoke and shit. I'll drink till I'm wasted but I don't wanna smoke. Who am I gonna chill with? ☹ Dude it's so fuckin cold here, I can't wait till I getta [get to] go to Florida! Aw shit I hope I still getta go. My grades suck ass b/c i'm always online and not doin my hmwk [[homework]]. I gotta do good on my next report card. :/. Aright well i'm gonna go finish watchin the Cleveland/orlando NBA game. I'll check back lata…

    ~Amy ♥

12/28/03

Hi.

I am in the worst mood. #1 Lily J left for vacation so I have like no one to talk to for the next week. #2 we just left to go back from my grandparents'. OK so I was walking out to put my stuff in the car and my Grandma stopped me and she was like 'next time you needa [[need to]] spend at least 5 minutes talking to me. You've barely said 10 words to me'. And she wasn't kidding either. She was speaking in such a harsh tone. So I go put my shit in the car and I'm like 'I've never seen Grandma that pissed' to my brother. Little did I know I hadn't seen anything yet. So I come out of my room and go into the kitchen and my mom says we aren't going to mighty taco anymore so i'm like why? I was all packed when you said I had be and idk we just kinda got into an argument. I didn't call her any names or raise my voice or <u>anything</u> but my grandma comes over and she fucken grabs my arm and she's like "do not talk to your mother like that. She is way more experienced than you and i wouldn't treat a dog the way you are treating her"! OK and this is fucking in front of all my cousins and aunts + uncles. Then my grandma starts crying and she's like 'i'm sorry' and then she's like 'i just can't believe you would treat your mother like that'. Then I leave and go to my room and apparently my mom and grandma were both crying so my little cousin is in my room and i start talking to him and i was seriously sooo fucken scared to go back out there. I talk to him for like 10 minutes and then my sister walks in and shes like 'you should apologize to grandma, I can't even look at you'. It's not fair, everyone knows that my brother, Dad, and even my sister occaisonally all talk to her much worse than that. But everyone feels all bad for grandma. It was gay. No-one cares about how I feel after that. Except my cousin. Remind me to like buy that kid like a car for his birthday. He is so sweet, he stayed w/ me the whole time I was in that room. Whatever I can't deal w/ this shit anymore. Im gonna write about my dream. Last night I dreamt that Elyssa Nebo and Lily J became best friends. And me and Katarina became best friends. Wanna know something else? Lily had the exact same dream last nite [[night]]. Weird huh? Kinda freaked me out a little. Idk I mean I wanna stay close w/ Lily J. but I also wanna meet new people. Oh yeah did I tell you? I might be stayin @ bvmp next year while Lily goes to RPHS. Partly to get away from her because she pisses me off a lot but I'd miss her a lot. I love judging ppl w/ her lol it sounds bitchy I know but it's fun. We split our grade into different names (code names). Whatever. Well. I gtg, my arms getting hella tired. I'll ttyl, thanks for listening.

 –Amy ♥

                      Jan 4th

Hey,

Hung out w/ Rosanne, Clinton, Audrey, Audrey's friend, Helmut, DL, Carlos and Hector for New Years. Drank a little mini bottle of alcohol. Dude I like hadda [[had to]] bullshit my way outta [[out of]] shit today.* I didn't do my labs but I told my mom I did so she came lookin 4 them. I hadda do 1 today while she was away. I bought caffeine pills for school. Dude my life's fucked up. I need rules but when I get them I can't take it.

And I am THIS CLOSE to tryin weed. Shit. + you know what else weres me out? How much I wanna be popular @ bvmp. I guess its cuz I was @ middle school and I loved it. But its not that easy @ bvmp. Its not just about wearin abercrombie and bein preppy. Its waaay hard to get popular and I guess thats why I want to keep up my rep as a badass b/c they all thinks itz cool that I get in trouble. If it weren't hard to b popular I wouldn't give a shit, but its like the things I want I can't have. O ya Audrey invited me to chill w/ druggies 2mrw. I think shes starting to suspect that I really don't do drugs so I gotta do something to make her think I do. I really miss Lily J. I wanna talk 2 her so bad. i am excited for school w/out her though. I think I'm gonna go now. Thanks 4 listening.

    ~Amy ♥

* Also Audrey invited me to come smoke 2ce but idk i just froze up and so i bullshitted and said I was tired…ugh…she must know I don't do it.

Jan 14th

Hey,

    Faked sick today. Thought I'd get more attention from it. I am like obsessed w/ getting attention. The other day we were @ class meeting in the auditorium. Lily got yelled at so I thought I had to match that so I went to the nurse and then I found out that a ton of people said I had 'mental problems'. Whatever, thats gay. I started taking pills. Caffeine and sleeping. I bring them to school and give em to Audrey and stuff. I let Ursula have my cell phone for the week, I hope she gives it back. I'm supposed to go away with Lily Feb. 6th because I told her I know how to snowboard last year even though I don't. Here's my plan (I can't blow her off cuz I've done that 2ce). The week after midterms on the weekend i'm gonna go to the doctor's because of my foot and i'll get crutches so every one will ask me whats wrong and then I'll still go away w/ Lily but I won't be able to snowboard but I'll still be able to meet her hott cousin. I found that I'm really horny. I was seriously considering asking Noah Labuan (my x) if he wanted to have a 1 nite stand w/ me sometime but he wasn't online. Idk like there are opportunities that I have but I don't feel good enough about myself to take them. This 18 year old guy, Raul, keeps calling me and asking me to chill but I keep blowing him off haha. Anyways….what's up? Dude yesterday after school Lily wasn't there so I hung out with Rosalyn after school. She's a cool chic [[chick]]. She told me shit like that [...] GAVE HEAD to 2 GUYS FOR $95 A GUY!!!! I was like holy shit…. then we ran around and tried to steal tests from all these rooms but there weren't any in there. OK idk where the fuck

Rosanne Ubangi is. She's been fuckin absent for like a week. She's cool but she's kinda suicidal so idk if she's in the hospital or what. I'm very worried. I am such a bitch. Just like in 'Cruel Intentions' (best movie EVA!) i have an: *Amy's back-stabbing world of friends*. I tell Lily shit about everyone. I tell everyone shit about Lily. She just pisses me off sometimes. I don't know if I want to be her friend sometimes but I realize that it will be 99999x worse if i'm not her friend b/c if there's 1 person good @ ruining ppls lives, its her. Then I told her how Loralee B was lyin to her about settin her up w/ this guy and so her + Loralee are totally in a fight now and idk I am such a bad person. I need some one fresh and new to talk to once and tell them all my problems and get help and then never see them ever again (b/c i wouldn't wanna face them after they knew how fucked up I am. Theres 2 sides to me. I wanna be a badass, a rebel, I wanna fuck, drink and smoke on 1 side, but on my other side I wanna get straight A's and go to Duke and be a great student. Shit my stomach hurts I think the sickness I faked today is coming true! Love yah!
    ♥ Amy

Jan. 15th

OMFG [[Oh My Fucking God]]. Okay so I'm on the phone watching tv right? and my parents come in and they're like "we're leaving in 10 minutes to go to your sisters concert". OMG. WTF [[What The Fuck]]. #1 I had no warning so I'm still in my fucken pajamas. #2 I am never in the mood to see ANYBODY ANYWHERE from RPHS let alone actually going to the school. #3 I can't fucking stand concerts, especially not fucking chorus ones so I'm like 'no i'm not going' and me + my parents get in this huge fight and I say I have a headache and I was sick yesterday and I just wanna study for midterms. So then my dad goes + shuts off the internet (GAY). So now I'm cooped up in my room. I dunno [[don't know]] what my parents are doing. Theyre probably calling up oh shit my mom just called me down… brb [[be right back]] (shit from then cleared, I stayed home to "study" and gotta miss it#)

Jan 17th '04'

Hey!

Just got back from babysitting… made $30. I'm using it for the mall tomorrow so I can buy stuff for the dress down day… idk why i care so much about having new clothes all the time. I guess it's because i want everyone to think i'm hella rich. My entire outside life is a lie. Oh well. Today was a good day so i don't wanna ruin it. My parents scheduled my spring Training trip (my b-day prez [[present]]). In total it's gonna be over $1500 (including food, hotel, tickets, hair braiding, etc…). This is the most I have ever gotten from anyone for any holiday! I haven't even lied about getting $1500 worth of stuff! I'm so excited….it's kinda weird though… i've been so mean to my mom lately, but my parents are still doing this for me "because we promised it last year". Ugh I really hate myself. I let anything distract me from studying for midterms! I found out that for the last week my friend Rosanne Ubangi has been in a mental hospital. Its weird cuz she always seems so happy about everything. She's suicidal tho. Fucked up shit in hischool. I haven't listened to any Tupac songs lately and he's my inspiration so i'm gonna go. LUV YA!

~Amy

p.s. I've been holding back from some of my real dilemas but I will get to them soon enough… I promise […]

Jan. 21, 2004[2]

Hey,

Before I start, I just wanted to say how happy I am to have you as a diary. It is the one place where I can be truthful. Today was good but at about 11:30 things changed. It is such a bad day. Ok so it all started at the mall w/ Lily & Audrey like a month ago. We got a bunch of random ppl's #'s including a guy named Raul. Like a week later I called him and we started talking. Like every day he invited me to come chill and smoke weed with him but I always blew him off, even though he's hott. Then last night I told him to come to our school (so I could show him off) and he did! Like OMG! Then the shit started. Audrey & I went out to see them while me & Lily were moving lockers (the principal was being a fucker…. I tried to put up a show for the cool people.. bad choice) anyways, Audrey comes in and she's all like 'they're waiting to meet you and smoke and shit' and I shoulda [[should have]] called it off then but i had a reputation to uphold so i was all like 'i needa ditch Lily i'll meet you in a few' and then i told Lily in private that i didn't wanna go so they kept following us and then i kept doing the same thing like tellin Audrey that 'I wanted to go, but Lily'll tell on me'. Idk I mean I wanna smoke but when it comes to the moment I just can't bring myself to do it. I ended up sneakin away from Audrey and getting out of it but tomorrow is gonna suck. I'll have to keep lying ☹ Lily's mad at me because I "got her involved". Whatever. […] I need to sort out my life. My birthday was yesterday. I got earrings (ugliest shits i've ever seen). a scarf (knitted by my sister….I was expecting a dvd but um.. okay), and a memo

---

2. Amy is 15.

book. Holy shit. Worst gifts in eternity this year no joke. I did get an $1000 Spring Training trip b4 my b-day that was HOT!

'- Just got back from watching the OC... i just have so much bottled up inside I wanna let it out but I can't.

mood: :-/ and tired

~Amy

Jan 27, 04'

Wow.

Today SUCKED ASS. OK well you know how I lent out my cell to Rosalyn and Ursula? Well they fuckin ran up my bill to $65! I had to pay back all of it... WTF. My mom is sooo pissed, because she thinks it was me that made all the calls during school and shit and I don't wanna tell her it was other ppl b/c then she'd prob. [[probably]] find out exactly who they were and it'd be wicked embarressing. I told her that $30 of the bill was from my friend's txt messaging but that just made everything worse. I hate this. thats $65 that I could buy 3 Aber. shirts with. WTF >:-o And then my parents are being fags and not letting me talk to the outside which is so fucken annoying – i hadda go up to bed @ fucking 10. To top that I got Lily + Loralee into an even bigger fight b/c I told Loralee Lily said shit bout [[about]] Rosalyn and then she told Rosalyn so now they're pissed but Rosalyn told fucken Lily so now Lor is pissed @ Rosalyn. UGH. Its all gunna come back & bite me in the ass. I just can't seem to stop lying. Anyway I haven't really written in a while so i'll fill you in on shit that's goin on. Raul doesn't call me that much nemore [[anymore]] b/c I blow him off like every day! Him & his friend Davy called me last night tho. Davy is black. Davy is 17. Davy does crack & weed (his Mom's a dealer). CAN YOU SAY SEXY? AHHH! ooo i gotta tell you about my trip. Well I called up Verizon Wireless over the weekend to see what my bill was at and when I found out how much $ it was I fucken FREAKED. I decided to pretend I was dying on bill day (today) so I'd live life to the fullest till then. I bought a fish & Oakleys behind my parents back and I decided I wanted a trip to FLA over Feb. vaca. My mom had already said no b/c I'm too 'disrespect-ful' so I decided to write a letter of apology to her and to my principal. IT WORKED! We got the tickets last night! I have to admit, I'm pretty good ☺. I got in so much trouble today though, my mom said she might cancel my tickets.....fuck. I try to be good but sometimes it feels like my parents (esp. [[especially]] my dad) are trying to purposely piss me off. Like today, they know I wanted to talk to Lily on the phone but they made me get off and practice violin and then go rite to bed. I fucking hate them. I made that pretty clear on my AIM [AOL Instant Messaging] away mesg lol. Anyways I'm gunna go now, I might re-read this diary for the 1st time ever, or just go 2 bed….idk. I will ttyL!

      ~ Amy ♥ smile of the day: raneka being realllllllly nice and friendly to me! ☺

Mood: >:-o

Jan. 29, 04'

I'm crying so hard right now
WORST FUCKING DAY OF MY ENTIRE FUCKING LIFE. I'm so upset and mad right now, I can barely write. OMFG. OK. I will start from the beginning. For the past 2 weeks Olivia has been out. Today I was talking to Tennise and everyone was like 'I can't believe u guys were so mean to Olivia'. Then @ like 2:30 today I was in the school library when Lily came in. She said 'did they tell u?' I said 'tell me what'. She explained how the school called her mom. Apparently Olivia and her family filed a restraining order against me & Lily (for harassing her). Sure we were mean, but she started it. Lily then announced that she's [FUCK my mom just picked up the phone when I was on the phone w/ Lily + i wasn't supposed to be] leaving bvmp and going to RPHS. I never thought I would care this much, but I actually started crying. I couldn't take it. This fucking sucks. I walked through the school crying and everyone asked what was wrong but I said 'nothing'. Then the dean came and asked what was wrong and she offered to sit down and talk to me. She is so nice. Then baddd shit happened. I was taken into a room with a cop, the principal, the president, and my parents. We had a long conversation about

----

OMFG. My parents just picked up when I was on the phone w/ Lily n [[and]] now they don't trust me + they took my cell away fuck. It has all my #s in it FUCK and it has weedman next to like all the #'s. FUCK ME. I FUCKING HATE THE WORLD

----

life sux [[sucks]] ☹ so sad i fucken hate Olivia
-Amy   mood >:-O
Laugh of the day: none

Feb. 4

This has officially been the worst week of my fucking entire life. I'll summarize it. Olivia situation, Lily left, Raneka left, my fish died and then came back to life, ppl are taking Olivias side at school, I lost my $300 palm pilot, I left my agenda @ my babysitters house, Raul stopped calling me, my cell phone got taken away and I have no will power to do any of my assignments so I'm fucked. I don't even know what to do. The weird thing is, i'm still in shock. I don't care that my palm pilot is gone. I have no feelings, no joke. It's scary. This has honestly been the toughest week of my entire life x100000. Why did this all have to happen this week? Why couldn't it be spread out? Oh yea and 2 more things. My comp. broke last night (my dad fixed it tho) and to top off all that I just got my period. A miracle did happen today though I came home at 1pm (long day) and I found my fish tank knocked over and all the water soaked out. IDK how long my fish went w/out water but I told my mom and instead of getting mad that I got a fish behind her back she was sad and she saved my fish b/c it still breathed ☺ Happy because of that. FUCK i'm tired, i'll tell u more 2mrw. I ~~LOVE~~ HATE Life. mood :"(

~Amy

laugh: Loralee in guidance office.

Feb 10, 04

Very little time to talk. It's 12:37. I am going to stay up all night doing work. I have gotten no rest. I am so stressed out. I can't take the pressure it's too much. Big weekend to talk to you about later but I have to get back to my work now, see ya.

–Amy

Hey. I'm a little calmer now. It's 2:45 am i took caffeine pills at like 10 and they didn't kick in till like 30 mins ago. I'm so awake now, but all my hmwks done so i got nothing to do. HOLD up i'm gunna switch pens.

Hey it's me w/ my pen still from Feb 10th. Well I guess it's the 11th now haha. OMG okay I have so many fucking problems but idk what I've already told. Lemme see… I pretended i hurt my foot so i could get out of snowboarding w/ lily (just b/c idk how to board and i said i did). And then @ school I had a convo [[conversation]] w/ Sally and i found out a lot of ppl r pissed @ me cuz i cheat on a lotta tests and shit. I wanna get into a great college but I know i can't but i'm trying. I'm way overworking myself. Oh well. That's life. And […] was gunna sell me cocaine and I gave her $ but now she 'can't find any' so she's giving me my $ back. Where do you have to go to get some good coke [[cocaine]] round here? No, i still haven't tried drugs, but i will snort any cocaine and eat any mushroom i can find (i don't wanna smoke anything just yet.) Wait – once i went out on my roof with a homemade pen pipe and like 1 nugget of weed and i tried to smoke it but it wouldn't work. Ugh and i stole this math test midterm for my friends cuz my moms the math teacher and i'm so fucked if ne1 tells, cuz like the whole grade knows. Lemme see.....oh yeah Lilys doing ok @ RPHS but she has no friends apparently. I feel kinda bad but w/e [[whatever]]. Oh yeah – did I mention i'm fuckin obsessed w/ ebay? I can't not go on ebay. good thing my dad put a block on the internet after 10:30 cuz otherwise i'd get absolutely <u>NO</u> homework done. Only 3 more days till i go to FLA. Get away from everyone; everything. OK well i'm gunna try to get to sleep now even though the effects of my caffeine pills aren't over yet. TTYL.

~Amy ♥

2-13-04
Friday the 13

There is now a new deffinition to the phrase 'worst day of my life'. Today my mother found the caffeine pills and the sleeping pills I've been taking. I also got another detention and the dean talked to my mom about me not retaking my test. I just got out of a 1 hr talk w/ my parents. I still think it's all a dream. My life is falling apart. I am being tested for psychological disorders March 8th and my parents signed me up for a shrink. Lily is away so I have no-one to talk to. I am so scared. I am seriously thinking about killing myself. I walked by my parents office and they were talking about how i spent my money and dad went 'well we know 1 way she spends it??' He was referring to the pills. Why are they concerned about how I spend my money? Idk what to do. My parents are gunna talk about further punishments. I know they're gunna go through my stuff when I'm in Florida. I hate life. Please kill me.

~ Amy

Hey-

I'm on the plane on my way to Florida I'm so excited! I'm getting away from everything. Wanna know something that's really weird? I was thinking about what would happen if the plane crashed, and I decided I didn't care if it did. Now that's fucked up. I've also been thinking a lot about my shrink that my parents are signing me up for. I know exactly what she's gunna do. She's gunna try to get everything outta me and then go tell my parents about it. Well I'm not tellin her shit. I'm gunna play the whole happy thing and pretend nothings wrong. It's all about the bullshit

☺. The only way I'm gonna tell the truth is if I'm sent to a psychiatrist instead of a psychologist. If that happens then I'm gunna totally blow my problems way out of proportion. That way they'll prescribe me pills! Like prozac! Woo hoo! So I told my mom that I want a shrink and she said she'd look into it. Omg though you wanna know something that made me soo happy? Both Raul and Helmut wanna chill w/ me. I know Helmut likes me and I think Raul just wants play but hes so cool and he's hell sexy. And today Raul called me up and he wanted to know if I wanted to hang and I was like okay i'll call Audrey and see if she can come but he just like 'no i only want you don't invite her!' That made me feel sooo special. Like my self esteem is so low right now so to hear something like that just makes me so happy. I know he just wants to fuck, but hey, he's a damn good persuader! Dude I'm sitting next to my mom while I'm writing this. If she read this I'd be sooo dead! Anyways we're about to land in DC and its turbulent ☺ so I gtg, I'll ttyl!!!

    ~ Amy

Hey –

    I'm at my hotel room in DC (we got bumped to a lata flight) and I can't sleep. I'm just thinking about boys and how much I miss having a boy-friend. I'm also thinking about sex. I think I wanna have sex soon. It's the horny side of me talking here. I'm thinking about calling Noah Labuan up and askin him if he wants to do a 1 night stand but idk. Last year Noah and I went out and went 2 3rd after $\underline{2}$ days. Then I dumped him, not cuz I didn't like him, but b/c he wanted to go to 2nd and I wore padded bras so I didn't want him to know I was small. Another potential guy is Ezekiel Qara. He's sexy, sweet, buff, and he can beat up like ne1. The only reason he doesn't have a g/f [[girlfriend]] is b/c he wasn't 'popular' last year. Well I think I'm gunna call him and see if he wants to catch a movie or something. See I don't wanna call him and ask for sex b/c he doesn't know me and I actually kinda want him as a b/f [[boyfriend]] whereas w/ Noah, I just wanna fuck. Ahh I sound like such a whore! W/e happens though, i'm gunna ask my mom 4 the pill 1st cuz i don't wanna get pregnant! Idk how imma [[I am going to]] do it, but I'll find a way.

    ♥ Amy

2/16/04

Heyy,

I've been in FLA for 2 days now. It was weird. yesterday I was walking to Burger King and this white van honked and i thought nothing of it but then they drove by again and honked again and when I looked there were like 2 20+ yr old guys and they waved at me! It might have been the fact that I was wearing slutty shorts and a tank top but I'm just a pale, skinny 15 year old with brown hair and small boobs. Oh well. They drove by again but I was in BK so they didn't see me. I've come to the point in my life where I have to dress up and shit when I go out b/c of guys. I wish I were a kid again– I wouldn't have to worry about shit like that. I also have to worry about strangers that try to take advantage of me b/c even tho I know its bad, I'd prob. let them b/c Im in all girls school and I need men! Oh yeah idk if I've told you, I wanna try coke and mushrooms. I was gunna do weed but I don't really wanna smoke anything. Coke would be awesome b/c you don't have to but I'm fuckin scared of OD-ing. Mushrooms would be sick too! They're a hallucinagen so they make you see things and they can last up to 8 hours!!! Holy shit if I took em' right b4 school I'd be soooo fucked up! Ahhhh! that'd be beautiful! Ugh I need a dealer though. Im gunna talk to […] and […] bout it (cuz they know dealers) and if they can't get me shit then I'll get sum from Raul. Ahhhh i'm psyched. Who knows I mite smoke sum weed after school […]. Oh yeah I think I might like a kid named Helmut. I think he's gay but he'd make a good boyf and he likes me sooo hopefully it'll work (even tho I blew him off on valentines day, the day after, and the day of his bday). Imma call up Rosanne and Clinton and see if we can all chill at Clintons <u>sum day</u> like Friday and maybe watch a movie. Then me and Helmut (I call him Tegu btw) can cuddle. I love boys. I don't wanna stay at bvmp any longer. I will fucking shoot myself if Olivia comes back. She has caused me so much shit. AHH. Like I'm emotionally scarred. Life sucks. I kinda got a little tan 2day [[today]] though. I'm gunna call Lily J now though so I'll ttyl!

~Amy

Sun. Feb. 29, 04

Hey,

I'm so sorry I haven't written in a while, there's just been so much going on in my life. Lemme just start off like the day I got back from FL. [[Florida]] to school. It was great. Every1 was saying how tanned I was and I was actually starting to make a lot of friends. Raneka Oberam was one of my closest, and we were really starting to get close last week. Ok so anyways, school's getting really hard, but apart from that Mon –Thursday afternoon were like the best school days for me so far. Ok but anyways Weds. afternoon Raneka tells me that she told guidance that Rosanne Ubangi did drugs, and was a dealer. So I was like um okay. First of all that's total bullshit because Rosanne U. has never even touched weed (she says she has but thats b/s [[bullshit]]). And 2nd of all, even if she did do drugs, she says she quit in September. Ok so anyways after school Weds. [this other girl] comes up to me & she's all like 'guidance just pulled me in and said they thought I did drugs and shit, did you tell on me?' and I was like 'no, OMG that was Raneka'. That was like the biggest mistake ever. So anyways after school Rosanne U. calls me and tells me that her and her rents' [[parents]] just got out of a meeting where Rosanne was being accused of being a dealor!!!! I was like OMG so I told her also that it was Raneka that told. So then I make them swear on their souls that they won't say anything to anyone about Raneka till I said so. So anyways the next day I got to miss part of school (1st 5 periods) b/c I was bein tested @ RPHS for ADD [[Attention Deficit Disorder]]. So then I told every1 I was out w/ ned and every1 believed me & I told Loralee B to come (I said ned was picking me up @ 7:45 from school) and so that morning her, rosalyn, elyssa, katarina, raneka, cleo kibo and a bunch of other ppl were lookin for his car! LOL! I'm so bad. So anyways when I got back Raneka and I were cool (like b4) but then she had a guidance appt. and thats when all the shit started. After French I came down + raneka was w/ Lenora L + Trudy. I went to talk to them and Raneka said 'I'm so mad at you Amy'. So then I found out apparently [...] + [...] told guidance that I told on Raneka and I got her in a lot of trouble. Then we all (Audrey, Rosanne, me, Raneka, Ms. Guicona [[Guidance Counselor]], the principal) had a meeting on Fri. morning about why there might be drug accusations and I stood up for Audrey the whole time but in the end she was like 'it was probly Amys caffeine pills'. I was like OMG! Then I started crying b/c my parents trusted me that I never brought pills to school and now I'm SO fucked.

But anyways onto new things. On Thursday night I decided I needed a man so I called all these guys (Rosanne U.'s friends) including a guy named Roy. Everyone was planning to go over Clintons on Friday so I was all excited but then my parents grounded me from it b/c of everything that happened @ school so I sat home all day + watched movies about drugs. It was fun I guess but @ Clintons Roy + […] hooked up. ☹ Its okay tho b/c I talk to Roy all the time online + he still wants to do stuff w/ me ☺ Hes supposedly <u>SO</u> sexy (blonde hair, blue eyes, 5'11) and he's a stoner. HELL YA! Dude but u wanna know what fucking sucks? I probly have to get a drug test done by a police officer at school, so I can't do any drugs till that happens but for all I know they could do it in like May. The good news about right now is that I can get so many drugs from ppl n Raphael Iduma can hook me up w/ weed & shrooms [[hallucinogenic mushrooms]] and he wants to chill w/ me same w/ Raul (he started callin again). And then Clinton has friends (Roy and Oswald) and Roy smokes weed and Oswald is a dealer, so basically rite now I can get hooked up w/ nething [[anything]] I want! I was so planning to eat some magic mushrooms b4 school one day but now I can't b/c i'll prob. get caught and then have a drug test done and my rents [[parents]] would KILL me! And this weekend was also a shitty weekend not to be able to go out b/c there are so many guys that I could hook up with. Theres Roy, Raul (he wanted to h/o [[hang out]] last night) Merritt (yes, Merritt Gibeon). He invited me over last nite lol). **Oh BTW – Audrey just QUIT DRUGS! WOW. This is depressing.**

3-1-04.
Wow. I thought life couldn't get any worse. Well remember how I said me + Loralee met up w/ Lyman + GW @ the movies? Well I thought Lyman mite have thought I was @ least ok looking b/c he was kinda chekin me out but today Loralee calls him up + you wanna know what one of the first things he said was? "Dude, Amy looks like a guy. If u gave her a haircut she'd seriously look just like me.' Wow. The thought of hearing him say that has put me into depression from 5pm till now. I don't know what it is but lately my egos been getting just a tiny bit higher. Maybe b/c of my tan. Maybe b/c of that guy approaching me when I went to the mall w/ Lily, or maybe it was just that I've been invited to a lot of guys houses lately but whatever my ego was it is now completely destroyed. My self confidence is in the fucking negatives. I'm sinking deeper into depression. I cut my arm today, with a ruler. Sometimes I wanna kill myself. I just can't deal w/ everything that's going on. The only happy world is the one

I lie to my friends about (Ned, big house, nice cars). Then my parents just put all these rules on that I can't have phone after 7. And I have a history project to do but I can't bring myself to do it. And I've never even tried drugs before (i can't get my hands on any) but I have a drug problem. It's psychological basically. I am obsessed with drugs. I just can't do this anymore. Like after everything w/ Olivia, Raneka, Rosanne, the drug thing @ school, my grounding, my grades sucking etc etc etc., lyman just put the icing on the cake. There isn't 1 thing in the world that I love, I mean really LOVE. No bad feelings or anything about. I'm so depressed. ☹

-Amy

3/4/04

Hey. Ah I'm confused idk if i'm happy or sad. I think I have bipolar disorder but I can't tell my shrink b/c idk why but I have a lot of trouble telling ppl I have friend / boyfriend probs. Ugh the sox played today and i imed [[instant messaged]] this guy Yasmine Piave was gunna date. Yasmine thinks she's higher than every1 + she pisses lotsa [[a lot of]] ppl off but 2day Freda Q was bring kinda mean, well we all were, and she pretended she didn't care b/c 'she knew it was a joke' but I swear I saw her eyes welling up. Anyways I'm so tired and I haven't done any hw. Ahh.

    -Amy

3/9/04

OMG really scared just got out of a HUGE fight w/ mom she fucking screamed at me for telling her i can handle my own life. Then I ran upstairs to try + get away from her and she followed me + started crying.[...] Ugh. Don't really wanna get into that though. So ya I watched requium for a dream 2day. It was disturbing + it depressed me. I still have so much homework ahead of me. Well I don't have much else to say so i'll ttyl.

    Amy

3-13-04

Hey,

    Today & yesterday have been interesting. Yesterday I talked to Byron on the phone for like an hour, and we're goin on a 'date' on Friday to catch up. I'm kinda excited because me & him have <u>so</u> much in common and it'll be interesting to see what happens…! I've worn a padded bra for like a while now but I think I'm stopping because it just restricts me from so many things, like swimming, tank tops, and even boyfriends… Speaking of boyfriends, I talked to Noah Labuan today. He IMed me online and I told him I'd call him tomorrow. Then tonight I talked to Freda Quilmes for like 2 hours and we called up this guy Galen who does weed and I'm kinda happy b/c I get to meet him in like 2 weeks. Anyways today has been like the happiest day for me in forever! Like the thought of having a relationship w/ anybody (Noah, Byron, even Galen) makes me so happy. When I'm in school I get so upset and depressed, but now that it's the weekend and I haven't had any commitments (babysitting, CCD [[religious education at church]]) I'm so happy. And when I'm sad I'm always SO tired but when I'm happy I tend to stay awake and it's like 12:30 (my longest night in a <u>WHILE</u> and I'm soo awake! Alrite [[all right]] well I gtg but I'll write soon!

~Amy ☺

3/14/04

Hey! Dude I decided my goal is to try weed b4 i finish this diary, or b4 I start my next 1. This weekend has been one of the happiest ever for me. I didn't let anything affect me. And I have 2 sets of plans. 1 w/ Byron (he'd come over next Friday) or I'd go to the movies w/ Freda, Galen, & Keith and smoke weed w/ Galen & Rex afta [[after]]. Can you believe I <u>still</u> haven't tried drugs yet!!! Hehe wow I've just had such a relaxing weekend… I hope I can stay happy this week ☺ Well neways [[anyways]] I'll talk to ya lata.

3/18/04

Snowday yesterday. Still haven't done my history paper. i'm so fucked over. Anyways I was just thinking about the year. At 1st I was totally happy w/ just Lily as a friend, but then when I started talkin to Elyssa + people I grew an obsession over being popular. I didn't do any homework, I lied about the stuff I've done, and I basically based my entire life around trying to get that crowd to notice me. Wow, that was stupid. Now I'm gunna tell you the thing I cringe @ and hate to say more than anything. I fucked over my college career, and basically the rest of my life, just to be popular in 9th grade. I mean you don't understand – if I wasn't purposely getting in trouble to impress people – I was thinking about what I was going to do to get attention next and like i'd talk REALLY loud about drugs + stuff so the cool ppl would hear. The worst part of all of that is it didn't get me any friends. Elyssa basically stopped talking to me, and like everyone else has shut me out and I think they all hate me. I have gotten a little better though. I've stopped caring as much as I did, but it's still a problem. It's exactly like Golum from Lord of the Rings. I have a good side that doesn't want any part of this trying to impress ppl thing but then theres this bad side that comes out on the spur of the moment. I would like to tell my problem but I do not have and will never get the courage to do so. I just wish I could start everything over. I'd do everything different. Oh great now I'm getting all depressed again. Oh yeah and now my shrink has requested a meeting w/ my whole family so now everyone's gonna know I see a shrink ☹. Well I wrote you b/c I was really upset about the whole life-ruining situation. Well I have to go now but I'll ttyl.

♥ Amy

3/30/04

HEY

　　　Sry [[sorry]] I havent written in a while. So much has happened. I don't know where to start. I saw the Red Sox this weekend [[at spring training]] in FL. It might have been the best weekend of the year and it might stay that way. I lied to my rents about my report card so its gunna come n i'll b fucked. And something weirds been happening. I have an unbelievable craving for drugs. Like i would give my left arm for 10 pills of ecstasy. Drugs are hard to get though. This girl [...] from school's gunna try n get me some but idk if shes full of shit. I need drugs tho. No1 [[no one]] can get them cept' [[except]] Raul but I don't really talk to him cause all he wants to do is fuck. N omg nekitas friend Miranda Tihuan got caught doing drugs n she got screwed over. Oh yeah Helmut (Tegu) asked me out. IDK what to say. But then he was pissing me off tonight so he said 'fuck u' to me n now im pist [[pissed (angry)]]. Oh yeah Galen is gunna come roll [[use MDMA, or ecstacy]] w/ me soon. All I wanna hear about nemore is drugs. I don't care about nething else. I'm fucking addicted but I still haven't tried any EVER! I have a huge rep though. I told every1 i'm in D.A.R.E. Holy shit dude. I'm tired imma go to bed. LUV YA.
　　　-Amy

March 31

Wow. Eventful Day. First off I lost my palm pilot. Like OMFG my brand new $200 palm pilot. (i found it tho ☺) How could I? ☹ ☹ Fuck. ☹. I'm gunna cry. Oh yeah Katarina's sellin me all this shit (drugs) but i deff. [[definitely]] think she's bullshitting bcuz [[because]] I kept asking her all these q's [[questions]] like 'how much' n shes like 'idk'. Lol. I outsmarted her - - she didn't know what florida snow [[cocaine]] was !!!!!!!! Hahaha. Funny shit. Oh yeah but I also had my family therapy today & my whole family was against me & my mom was all acting like a victim & shit. WTF. I hate her. Holy shit and I also realized I miss Lily. I'm fucking tired & sad. I'll tty more about it later. Cya.

April 2nd
Hey. [...] OMG I hate Elyssa [Nebo]. [...] When I was talking to Katarina (her BFF) for like 1 minute at lunch she walks by n' gives Katarina a look like 'why r u talking to her?' So now I'm gonna give her dirty looks. I can't believe I like tried so hard to be her friend - - I HATE HER! Oh yeah but now you see I have a lot more willpower to do work (schoolwork) so I'm actually staying for extra help now instead of sucking up to ppl I thought were my friends. Yeah and omg Loralee found out I "do drugs" and shes all like 'do u?' im like NO! She's a good friend but I think we're kinda drifting. [...] I don't want to tell my shrink why i'm sad (my paranoia) b/c I don't wanna sound like a loser but I hate telling my friends i'm ever sad b/c I hate ppl that just want attention for being sad n I don't want to be like that. Well igg [[I gotta (have to) go]] blow-dry my hair. TTYL (I'll write more tonight).
    -Amy

4/4/04
Heyy.. I'm layin in bed watching Requiem for a Dream. I just got off the phone w/ Helmut (Tegu). He's such a sweetheart. I think I might like him just a little bit. It's weird b/c I haven't liked ne1 since RupertJ which was in the summer. Clinton n Rosanne always tell me he's obsessed w/ me n he lies n says he does drugs just to impress me. That's sweet and @ first I thought I liked him just cuz he liked me but we talked for 101 minutes tonight and he's just awesome. All I need to do is figure out if I love him to pieces as a friend, or more. Oh yeah and holy shit I got shit to tell you. OMG so Rosalyn asked me if I wanted to buy her bowl cuz shes getting searched for drugs cuz she got caught so I said yeah but I didn't have the $ on me so I went down n had my mom give $40 to her for it (i said it was for sweat-pants). Fuck it. I feel so bad tho. I mean I used her $ towards drugs. I'm gonna have to live w/ the guilt for fucking ever. Fuck. ☹.
    -Amy

4-9-04

Hey... it's like 10:15 and i'm really bored. Recently I've had a lot of trouble at school. Me and Lily called Tennice D and left her a couple prank messages on her cell which she took REALLY seriously and she basically told every1 shit about us being bitches so now ppl hate me even more. OMG though, 2day Loralee B. called me up n she's like 'amy do u do drugs' n i'm like 'No' n she's like 'God could u stop lying for a second?' so then i found out that a lot of ppl (Elyssa, Katarina, etc.) told her i do drugs but i told them not to tell her. lol. wow. i don't give a shit. i'm so fucking sick of everyone. Also I'm wicked uptight cuz I paid Rosalyn $40 for weed and she still hasn't given me it yet. WTF. GAY. I don't need anyone, I'm so bitter but IDGAF [[I Don't Give A Fuck]]. Cya! ☺

~Amy

4-10-04

Hey. Wow um i'm fucked. Lol. Last nite I had Lily IM Loralee n b like 'so what if Lily does drugs?' n shit like that. NOW Loralee is like <u>REALLY</u> pissed at me, n she's tellin EVERYONE n now everyone's totally pissed at me lol. Oh yeah she's also telling every1 that when we were friends I only used her for some1 to sit w/ at lunch and that I broke up her n Lyman's friendship and all this other bullshit. Oh well. I'm sick of her neways. In some ways I wanted her to b mad at me (that's y [[why]] i made Lily IM her). Ay yai yai. I might fake sick tomm. [[tomorrow]] so I don't hafta [[have to]] go ta [[to]] church. Idk what to do cuz EVERY1'S iming [[Instant Messaging]] me n callin me n sayin 'r u on drugs?' shit. Can't wait for school on Monday... im gunna go now TTYL. A police officer is comin 2 adress the class.

~Amy

4-12-04

Hey. OK a lot's better now. Loralee called n said she was sry and Rosalyn called and left a message for me to call her which means she hopefully didn't 4get [[forget]] about the weed. ☺ Oh yeah every1 hates me – Lenora Liao is a fucking fag... w/e. Ah shit i'm so fucking scared b/c i'm so fucked if my rents find my bowl when i'm in South Carolina... holy shit like i've had dreams about getting caught doing drugs and i like kiss the ground when i wake up b/c they're just so scary! Oh my my my. Lol. Well I've got a lot of tests to study for so i g2g but i'll ttyl bye! ~Amy

4/16

Hey! I'm in SC [[South Carolina]] right now. At first I was havin a shitty time but now I'm really enjoyin it ☺ My aunt is so cool. Like she has all these wicked interesting stories to tell me, like about her job as a hospital doctor person and I just asked her about drugs and she says that they get a lot of patients that OD on ecstasy. She seems like a really good mom cuz she has stories about her experiences in high school and she's so sweet. Oh yeah OMG today Rosalyn called me n' invited me to hang out w/ her!!!!! I'm not totally sure but I think I'm gunna b/c she told me to call her on Monday when I'm back from here. I've never smoked and I think that's what we'd be doing but hey i'm cool w/ that. i've been waiting to try weed for sooooooo long! And also i'll have like a friend @ bvmp lol. Idk if i'm staying next year but it'd be good to have a friend if i do. Well idk we prob won't even talk after she gives me the weed but it's all good! Oh yeah also I think I have OCD [[Obsessive Compulsive Disorder]], i wrote down the symtoms in my palm pilot. OMG yeah 1 last thing - - for seriously 4 nights in a row I've had the same dream; that my mom and/or the school catches me w/ drugs. They always find either coke or my bowl. Shit. I hope it doesn't come true!!! I kno [[know]] drugs r bad but i wanna tryem [[try them]] once – just <u>ONCE</u> to see what they're like!!! I've totally been thinking about my adjustment … Like from being a kid to being a teen is so big, i thought it'd all be the same, but it ain't! Talk more about it lata.

      ♥ Amy

Hi there. Wow i had an interesting night tonight. My cousin Wade took me & 2 of my other cousins Mary and Samuel out to this place which had like go karts & arcade games & all this other shit. Until now I never realized how depressed I was cuz I thought it was all about being sad but I was so self-concious about how I looked and I thought everyone there was laughing at me even tho no1 even noticed me, but yeah I wouldn't go on ne of the rides or anything. But 1 really weird thing did happen me & Mary were waiting for Wade and Samuel to come outta the b-room and this guy (like 20-30s) came up to us at this like dance machine n he was like "go on i'll watch" n he like touched my arm n i was like OMG n Mary was like 'I'm scared' lol n then he was staring @ us for like another minute n then Samuel and Wade came back n the guy looked so scared like that we'd tell!

4/20/04

Hey,

Just got back from SC. Wade is the MAN. He was gonna take me to get my permit (but then we found out i needed all this shit to get it) and then he was gunna take me to get my fucking belly button pierced!! The only prob. was the place said i needed a doctors note if i was under 16. God I Love wade.. Anyways I've been thinking a lot about my depression. I'm so self concious that I don't even like going to the mall anymore, or anywhere in public for that matter. I live in my own little hole and when I come out of that hole I think I know the whole world hates me and they're judging me at every second. I won't try any teams in fear that i'll fail. I think it's from always being put down at the least expected moments By Lyman, Rosemary, Pedro….Instead of spending all my money on brand new clothes i spend it on electronics to make my own little world better. Every time I buy something I think it will make me happy but it never, ever does for more than 2 days. It's like I know I have no chance w/ the outside world, so why not make my world the best it can be. Another thing I wanted to talk about was Lily. I kinda feel like i'm losin her. All she cares about is how she looks and she won't come to 6 flags w/ me when it is raining b/c she doesn't want her hair getting frizzy. I just want a friend who could care less what they looked like when they go out. Someone who's world doesn't revolve around having Abercrombie clothes. Right now i don't want any friends.. idk why, but I just want a break from the world. I don't want that competition i feel every time i hang out w/ Lily. Well i guess that's life. If high school's supposed to be the best years of my life then what the fuck is the rest of my life gunna be like??? Neway i'm going to bed now…ttyl.
    ~Amy

4/24/04

Hey. Today was weird. Kinda fucked up actually. I talked to Rosanne Ubangi on the phone for like 2 hours - - she was really depressed about Clinton (her boyf) b/c he like ½ dumped her. Then I talked to him for like 20 mins and I was like flirting w/ him… I'm such a sick person and I hate myself. So neways later Rosanne IMs me online n she's like 'i'm going to the hospital' so I call her n she tells me she OD'd on advils n her dad found her cuts (from her slitting her wrists) so she's gonna get her stomach pumped n then she's gonna go to the mental hospital again probly. As I said – fucked up. I don't feel too bad tho b/c even though she's my friend I think she does some shit like cutting to get attention. Speaking of which, today I got in another fight w/ my rents' n i got so pissed I went upstairs n started slicing my left wrist, first w/ a protractor, then w/

a razorblade to make it bleed more. I'm not gunna do it again though cuz i don't wanna get caught. Oh yeah n i talked to Helmut again tonight… he's gunna come on the walk 4 hunger w/ me! i'm wicked excited. I think I might like him - - just a little bit. He's so nice & even tho he's not the most attractive guy ever i'd give him a chance if he asked me out again ☺ Well that's all for tonight. Cya.

    ~Amy

4/25

Hey. I think I like Tegu. We talked a lot today n i deff felt sparks. We made all these plans like to go to the mall n the walk for hunger n stuff. Only prob. is i think he's tryina [[trying to]] make me jealos [[jealous]]. b/c he always talks bout [[about]] otha [[other]] girls. Actually maybe he just don't like me nemore. Aw well. Talked to Fredas b/f Rex 2day - - he told me to call him 2mrw yay! He's nice. Also I'm really into sk8-boarding [[skate-boarding]] n my mom mite get me new stuff soon. yay. I've kinda been not focusing on drugs 2 much nemore so that's good.

    ~Amy

4-26

Hello. Hard day. When I got to school I went right up to guidance but Mrs. Guicona wasn't in and then I started to cry and have a panic attack but my mom wouldn't let me go home and then I got yelled at to go to homeroom. I hate school. Anyways when I got home I didn't get to sk8board. Later I got in a fight w/ Freda & Loralee about something stupid. Then I started to cut. I don't stop cutting till I see blood. Its like now I look fwd to 3 things when I get home: skateboarding, talking to Helmut, and cutting. Earlier this month I was trying to get myself depressed on purpose, but I think now that I did it, it sucks. I'm sad <u>all</u> the time and I feel like crying a lot but I don't know what's getting me this way. Suicide has been crossing my mind more n more lately. I was seriously considering ODing today but i didn't. Something else sad is that u & me are the only 2 in the world that know about my cutting and stuff. Half of me wants to tell someone so I can get out of this state but part of me will absolutely hate me if I do get help… cutting is just the way i deal w/ my problems and i don't want ppl knowing + judging me. Well I'm gonna go 2 sleep now. I will write later.

4/27

Holy fuck. My mom just saw my arm. i'm so fucking stupid she's the one person i didn't want to fucking see SHIT OMG Now i can't cut nemore. I'm an idiot i shoulda kept my wristbands on now idk whats gunna happen. What if she tells someone like my dad or my shrink? I lied n told her it was from skateboarding but she knows im fulla [[full of]] shit omg i'm in shock i wanna cut more but i can't i hafta fight it n i took caffeine pills an hour ago so now im gunna be awake for a long time. Takeing DEEP BREATHS thinking about how i need to talk to Miss Guicona. I hate 27ths or 28ths. They've all sucked. Shit shit Fuck.

    -Amy mood: scared/mad ☹ @ myself ☹

5/5/04

Hey. A lot's happened since b4 but idk if i wanna talk about all of it cuz it makes me mad. Lets see… in a nutshell my mom told my dad & my shrink about my cutting n it was bad. I went to the walk for hunger w/ Tegu it was fun. He made me feel good about myself for 1nce [[once]]. He kept telling me i was hot n he was like tryina stick his fingers up my pus** when he was giving me piggy rides. Idk…but then I got depressed again tonight, here's the story. So i IM Roy rite? N he's like i'm with clinton, Carlos, and DL. Then he's like 'Clinton says u look like a man. Is that true cuz if it is I don't wanna meet you'. I just can't do this. He's the 2nd guy that thinks that (Lyman too). Like I can't help the way i look… I'm so ugly my self-esteem is at a low right now n when ever it comes up just a little bit something happens n it just shouts back down again, ☹ Oh yeah n I got in another fight w/ Tennice Diamant so now the whole grade hates me even more – i don't have a place in this world idk if i should go 2 bvmp next year (or RPHS where every1 knows I wear a padded bra & hates me), or […] where Tegu is, but idk) … I'm so sad. If there really is a God, please forgive me for my sins and help me out of this emotional hell. Let me see what else is happening … I called this guy up n he's sellin me weed hopefully. I'm gunna see if he can meet me at the mall but idk. I'm so sad like when I wasn't depressed i wanted depression so i could get pills but now that i am depressed i hate it. I'm seeing a real pill prescriber on the 25th. Jeez i'm sad ☹

To talk about next time: I keep avoiding ppl cause I can't be myself around ne1. Evokes anxiety.

5/8/04

Hey. OK so heres whats happened over the past couple days. Yesterday I went to the sox game with Lily. it was kinda boring but then these guys apparently saw lily n they came up n talked to us … well i was doing most of the talking cuz lily didn't wanna show them her braces. Neways I got their #. Then lily wanted it in the car but i gave her a fake #. I hate myself. I think i'm just so defensive cuz i wanna be the experienced one in the friendship..

cuz she kinda looks up to me. OK so then today i went to the library and lily met me there at like 4 and she told me that her and her mom got in a fight n when she told me why i thought i was gunna bawl. She said that ever since me + lily have been friends lily's changed and that i have a horrible influence on lily. She said that i'm just like Evie from the movie 'thirteen'… that i need someone to cling onto and since that person is lily right now she says that i'm purposely getting people to hate lily cuz i don't want her having any friends other than me…n then she topped it off by saying that she didn't want lily hanging out w/ me and it was for the best that she left me at bvmp and if she was gunna keep hanging out w/ me she was gunna end up @ Canalboro University. Wow… that's all I can say. I don't even know what to think like Mrs. Jackson was so nice and i'm just in shock. Maybe that is what i'm doing… maybe i'm just a bitch but i have absolutely nobody to talk to becuz I don't want my reg. friends not hangin out w/ me now n i cant talk to svetlana about it cuz she still thinks me n lily r stepsisters n i can't talk to my family cuz its too embaressing. Also, no matter who it is… i hate telling people my sad stories cuz I hate people feeling bad for me and i don't want ppl thinking i'm boring 2 talk 2 ah idk. i don't think i want to hang out w/ lily anymore … i'm so scared of her mom.

5/14/04

Hey…Sorry for not writing, I've been busy w/ school work. Anyways not too much has happened. Me & Lily have kinda been disinigrating. I just keep letting my jealosy take over… like i hate the thought of her having a boyfriend when i'm a single, disgusting piece of shit so i try to get her to repel guys. She just got her hair redyed and she looks like a model- -she's gorgeous… like i'm so jealos cuz she was so ugly and now shes like way pretty. And things with school have gotten so bad I can't stay focused for 5 frickin minutes. I'm a total slacker. Last year I slacked off and it was the cool thing to do but this year doing your work is cool. I mean Terrill Viatka is on the honor role. Monica Raab is on the honor roll. Pedro Naas is on high honors. I need to get out of bvmp because it's absolutely killing me academically. I really want to go to Tegu's school… so bad.. I wouldn't be at bvmp with hard work, mean teachers, and no studies; but I also wouldn't have to be at RPHS where people are threatening to ruin my life, and where i have shit with (literally) everyone but 2 people. I need to write a letter to my parents about that. Oh jeez. I'm getting to the age where i can't talk about my self and my problems to ANYONE but you, my shrink, and my mom. Whenever I talk about me to ne1 else I feel like I'm weighing them down with my shit, and that makes me feel awful. I wish I had a happy life again. One where I didn't care that I had no boobs, acne, or a small house. All I care about now is what other people will think about whatever I do. I've thought about killing myself a couple times from all the pressure. The only reason I don't cut any more is because i'm scared my violin teacher will find it and tell my mom. Oh my gosh. My heart is so full of anger and jealosy I can't take it. OMG—I haven't had a boyfriend since Rupert J 9 months ago. 9 MONTHS! OMFG. This is horrible. Why do I hafta be so ugly? Whats going on in my brain? I hate myself. Thx 4 listening.

–Amy

5/21

Hey. Just got off IM w/ Roy… I think I mite like him! I mean I wouldn't go out w/ him bcuz he's a little player! But seriously like he's a total flirt! We were supposed to meet up today but I blew him off. We mite meet up this Sunday at the mall… I need some mini skirts. Gosh I'm so nervous… like I need this for my self esteem. Lemme see… this week I went to therapy n there was this guy n I swear he was molesting his sons. He kept telling them to sit on his lap n they'd be like 'dad stop'. They were like 7 & 9. I started cutting a little bit. I'll write more tomm.

-Amy

5/25

Holy Shit. I had my appt w/ a real psychiatrist today. I made a HUGE mistake. I told her about my cutting. Then she called my mom in n told her! I'm so fuckin pissed. When i wouldnt show the shrink my arm she was like "if u don't show me we cant work together—i'll refer u to someone else'. BITCH! I told my mom it was back in Jan when i did it, and the most recent scratches "really are from skateboarding". My mom hasnt said anything about that to me but theres tension between us. Oh yeah - - Roy and I are still talkin. We mite meet @ the mall on Friday. Let's see…what else? Oh, me & Lily are looking @ summer camps together. I can't decide if I wanna go 2 the same 2 as her. I mean I do cuz I want to have @ least 1 friend, but I don't want her knowing I wear a padded bra. Today I got so mad cuz she ditched me on the phone to talk to a guy about her proj [[project]] w/out even telling me! Thats so rude! Am I mad or just jealos? I'm so tired, I'll write lata.

♥Amy

5/26/04

Hey… Today i started takin my Zoloft. It made me super drowsy. OMG i went to fuckin therapy 2day …. my psychiatrist TOLD MY THERAPIST ABOUT MY CUTTING. OMFG. You know what I was thinking about today? OK i basically fuckin faked my way into depression to get these pills. B4 9th grade I was a happy kid w/ NOTHING wrong with me but today I'm a fucked up kid w/ no friends, and with depression medicine. I wanted to be sad so I could get the happy pills. Now that I'm sad my life sucks. There's actually one good thing rite now tho. Roy. I talked to him a little bit more 2nite… Well we probly talked for an hour, total. He reminds me a lot of Niko. He asks me questions like Niko, he flirts w/ like a billion other girls like Niko, he has like the same overall attitude as him… I hope he thinks i'm @ least a little pretty. Hey u kno what I just realized? I've been skippin church for the past couple weeks n i actually went this week n I've been havin a good week exept' for the whole shrink thing. ☹. Ugh, I wish I kept a diary when I was cheatin on Horacio w/ Niko… that's the interstin shit, not my depression. Imma take pics of Roy on Fri. I'm so excited! ☺ Wish me luck.

    ~Amy

5/27

Hey. […] I'm mad at Roy. Our mall plan got complicated so he's like 'im never gunna meet u, screw it' n so I think hes implying he doesn't have time 4 my bullshit. I mite like Helmut again. I feel so bad 4 Helmut right now cuz he's <u>REALLY</u> depressed and he cuts himself and stuff. I just want to tell him AND the WORLD how addictive it is to cut. In a way, I miss cutting but in another way i am <u>so</u> thankful i got caught because if i didn't i'd probly still be doing it right now. I don't wanna be on Zoloft anymore. I miss being sad o well. Back to Helmut- i invited him over for tomorrow… i think its just my hormones kickin in but i just wanna hook up with <u>SOMEONE</u>. […] Well i'm tired i'm gunna read Chickin Soup. [[the book *Chicken Soup for the Teenage Soul*] i'll ttyl. ♥ Amy

5/29

Hey… I'm writing on Sat. morning. I have so much h/w [[homework]] to do this weekend but Tegu came over last night from like 6:30-9:30. It was weird. Like 1st: b4 he came i had an away msg that said: "Tegu is comin over" or something n later when I came back Roy IMd me n he was like 'whos Tegu' n he was all pissed. OK 1st of all we're not goin out n 2nd – I thot [[thought]] he didn't wanna meet up nemore!! Whatever. Oh yeah OK so when Tegu was over I wanted to do something physical. I got him to lay down in my bed w/ me n i was like rubbin up against him n we kept flirtin n shit… so now i feel kinda like a whore. I decided I <u>NEED</u> to go to a CO-ED school. Like I would seriously do stuff w/ ANY guy that came over i'm so desperate! Gotta go work.. i'll write lata. ♥ Amy

5/30

Hey – Don't have that much time to talk but good day today. I got <u>ALL</u> the Degrassi spoilers so im hella psyched. Also, I got things better w/ Roy n we talked for like an hour today about like how far we've been n shit… Ahh I'm so confused!!! I think i like him but IM NOT SURE! Rents left me home alone ALLLL day 2day n I was gunna have peeps ova [[over]] but i decided not to because i don't want my rents' losin trust in me. […] O yea when Katarina said she wanted 2 chill i called up Raul 2 go 2 n HE CALLED BACK n he wants to hang out <u>STILL</u> even tho i totally blew him off like 2034897 times!!! Anyways today was a great day but i NEED to get my sci project done tomorro cuz im fucked if I don't! Alrite well cya!

 ♥ Amy

6/4

Hey – supposed 2 go 2 Roys earlier but his 'mom grounded him' so i couldn't go. Then I was supposed to go to the mall w/ Raul rite after school but He blew us off. I was <u>all</u> ready to smoke weed n shit n then he said he couldn't come something came up. I went to the mall w/ Rosanne n Audrey but they kept purposly ditching me so I had my mom pick me up (after waiting in Target alone for them for like half an hour). I did see Katarina & her boyf there. Dude everyone (Terry, Katarina, Audrey, Rosanne, Rosalyn) said they like my shirt tho so i'm HAPPY ☺. Gtg… tired…

 ~Amy

p.s. Loralee B n I made up from our fites [[fights]] n i found out ALL the soph's hate me

Hello diary – it's the summer FINALLY!!! Wow its been great with you. I've been so happy to have you as my diary. You have been here for me <u>all</u> the time. When no1 else would listen – you would. You've kept me sane. Anyways, it's the end. Thank you. I love you

 ♥ Amy

By the way – so we don't leave with unanswered q's – i went over Roys 2nite and I gave him head. It was weird. Alright I'll cya!

Amy wrote the title of the book, *Go Ask Alice*, in the inner cover of her purple suede journal.

However, she knew about the book around fourth grade, as seen in the following note found among her school papers.

Cutting Poem

....

Amy did not write a lot of poetry, but this poem was on a loose sheet of paper in her journal

6/7/0?

Can't stop
Its taking me over
Temptation... I need to do it

As i cut deeper and deeper the
blood gashes, beaded lines take over my arm
My arm is ripped apart
skin torn and rough

why does this make it better?
it doesn't. My pain will never fade.
Nothing, no1 can stop it...

I feel relieved
My arm is mutilated
I must live with the scars
but i can't stop. i can't stop.

im sorry

Four
Pink Fuzzy Notebook
(summer after ninth grade)

June 10th 04'[1]

Hey! This is a continuation from my old, purple diary. I've just completed my freshman year at BVMP. It was probably the hardest year of my life. Finally, summer started! Okay so let's see… right now I'm "going out" with this kid Wilhelm. I don't even know this kid… he went out with my friend Rosanne Ubangi n he was freakily obsessed with her n then she dumped him n then he asked me out. Dude I mean he's nice n everything but I don't want to be with him! We're meeting at the mall this Saturday, ugh! Anyways, throughout my life I've had 1 <u>really</u> sweet, caring boyfriend Niko. I had like 7 others but they didn't even compare to what I had w/ Niko. Like I could be totally relaxed on the phone with him. I didn't feel like I had to start conversation w/ him. We broke up after he cheated on me with my best friend, Evangeline. After that (late 8th grade) it was hard to find someone like him. OK, back to life now. I went over this kid Roy's tonight. Oh my goodness I really think I like this kid. We'd been talking since about February n I met him for the first time tonite. It was kinda awkward at first - - I was sitting on his bed for like 30 mins while he was on a chair but then we ended up flirting. He tried to lift up my skirt so he could eat me out but I said no and he respected that. Well I didn't exactly say no, I just told him I had my period, lol. I <u>REALLY</u> want to be eaten out but I didn't want him to see my birthmark. [[Amy had a smaller-than-dime-size birthmark on her outer thigh that always embarrassed her; she often covered it with a band-aid]] So anyways, then I was like 'how bout I do it to you' n he was like OK! I was really nervous because he had gotten head so many times and I'd never given it (even tho I lied to him n said I did). […]Anyways, I had to go n his Mom called us before I was finished. Oh well. Then wen we got back dressed n stuff he was bein so sweet. I sat on his lap for like 10 mins

---

1. Amy is almost 15½.

n he just hugged me n it was the best feeling in the world just to be held by him. ☺. His mom drove me home n on the way home he held my hand the whole time. Then when I got back home he actually called! I was expecting him to be like 'I'm not callin her' but he did. Oh man I just love him…♡♡ I shouldn't say that - - I don't love him but I like him for sure. I'm hoping things will work out between us. I just can't believe I gave him head!!! Ah!!! I'm like… I don't even kno. I can't wait to tell my friend Lily or Rosanne…Oh jeez. This is the happiest I've been FOREVER! TTYL!   ♥ Amy

June 11th 04'

Hey,

　　　I'm getting ready to go babysitting. I've been thinking about Roy all day today. He called this morning n we talked for a little bit. Its like so awkward on the phone.. I really wanna see him again. I like him a lot.[...] OK. Well I'm gonna go babysit now - -I'll ttyl!

Hey!!! OMG! Roy asked me out! I'm in total shock! I'm <u>so</u> happy!! I'm in total shock rite now! I'm the happiest I've been since I got Jason Variteks autograph for the first time! I am the girlfriend of the boy I like! And he told me he thought I was hott the first time he saw me ☺ ☺ ☺ I have been smiling all day (well since he asked). This is probly the best day of my entire life! N Roy ended the convo by sayin he loves me! N he called like 5 minutes later so I knew it was really him that asked me out ☺ I feel like I'm in a coma rite now… my life is so wonderful. I'm gunna go to sleep now … dream of Roy ☺ Goonight!
　　　♥ Amy

June 12th, 2004

Hey! Today I went to the mall w/ Loralee, her bro, and her friend. We met up w/ Wilhelm quickly - -he's better in person than pics/phone. When we left, I called Loralee n she was like 'my friend thought you were cute' n then she said something that hit me. She said 'but I was like too bad dude she has a boyfriend'. Wow. I do have a boyfriend. Omg I love Roy. He's just so awesome ☺ Me, him, Loralee, n his friend Calvin are all hopefully going to the movies tomorrow to see Shrek 2. Ugh. I need to end it with Wilhelm, but I'm so scared to because I feel so bad ︵. This 2-timing thing is hard and it sucks! I think I'm just gunna tell Wilhelm that I don't know him enough n i need time to think. Oh I feel horrible ︵. Oh yea I decided that me and Roys song is 'tiny Dancer' by Elton John. It makes me think of him cuz i played it <u>all</u> nite yesterday (when he asked me out). OK well there isn't much else to say…I'll write again tomorrow!
　　　♥ Amy

June 13th, 2004

Hey! It's been a long, eventful day. OK, where should I start? I went out to breakfast with Loralee, Byron, my mom, my sister, and Kalli, who used to work for my mom. Then me & Lorall met Roy at the movies. He gave me a huge hug right when I got in. It's the best feeling in the world to be hugged by someone you love. Anyways, we saw a couple girls from school helpin out w/ the Jimmy fund (Helena, Jasmine Piave, & Terry) so having Roy made me feel even better. When we went in Roy had his arm around me n he fingered me rite in front of poor Loralee! Neways we ended up goin to 1st (makin out), 2nd (feelin boobs), 3rd [...] and sloplly 3rd [...]. I didn't like it at first but i'm pretty sure that's just because I wear a padded bra n I don't want Roy findin out. Neway, I was about to make him cum [[come]] but then Loralee came back ∵. Roy n I talked on the phone for like 2 hours tonight. He always tells me how beautiful I am, and calls me names like babe, sweetie, and (my personal faves) honeycakes. I really like him. Oh yeah I told Wilhelm we're taking a break cuz "Loralee likes him". so at least now I only have 1 boyfriend. I've met Roy 2ce in my life but it seems like I've known him for years. Oh yeah Byron Faenza asked me out online a couple hours ago… he knows i have a boyfriend but (ugh) i told him i wanted to break up w/ Roy (even tho I don't). I don't know what it is but I see Roy as a have-fun-playtime boyfriend, where as I see Byron as someone I could actually marry. I know it's crazy but idk… I just feel so natural around Byron. Ugh U kno I was so lonely and in need of a boyfriend durin the school year, n i had no1. Every guy I've wanted in the past like 2 years is comin to me now (all at once!). Also the first guy I ever kissed (Irving) wants to come chill with me in july… OMG! I miss him, but I have too much on my plate rite now, lol. I don't know what to do, I'm not used to getting all this attention from guys. not that it's bad, i'm just getting very confused ∵. It's kinda keepin my mind off drugs tho, so that's good. Oh yeah Roy said I love you on the phone (1st time ever on the phone) tonite. That made me feel so good. I'm gunna get to sleep. TTYL!

♥ Amy

June 14th, 2004

Hey… bad day 2day. I think Roy might be using me…he wants to have sex the day before I leave for Hawaii which is the 22nd. That's 11 fucking days after we started going out. I'm going over his house tomorrow, n he wants to go up my shirt (which means he'll find out I wear a padded bra. Ugh. I like him a lot but idk… he's almost deff. using me. Wilhelm called today n he was like 'after talking w/ Loralee I don't wanna see you anymore'… I was like 'ummm... okay'... he told Loralee she was gorgeous. In a way I'm like the tiniest bit jealos ... but idk. Byron was talking to me online today...he was like 'i like u'. But then he got rite into how far I'd go with him & shit... Oh jeez I'm getting really depressed. I'm not in the most talkitive mood so I guess I'll just write tomorrow.

     −Amy

June 15th, 2004

Hey... I don't even want to write I'm so upset. Tonight I went over Roys and things went too far. We were just messing around at first but then he [...] for a couple seconds (unprotected). Idk what I was thinking, but I'm so scared right now... What if i'm pregnant? OMG i hope not. I am going to church tomorrow to pray. I would kill myself if I were pregnant. I hate myself. Bye ☹.

June 17th 2004

Went to the mall w/ Audrey today. We snuck out to Harvard square 2ce. We met 3 guys our age (Chester, Larry, & Malcolm) n we walked n talked w/ them & their friends (Mutt + Jepp) for like 2 hours. The black guy (Larry) supposedly liked me n he kept asking me if he could kiss me n putting his arm around me n stuff. He's nice but he's just not my type. Like he tried too hard. He'd be an awesome friend tho. I'd probly be more interested in him if his buddy Malcolm wasn't there. I'm like <u>so</u> into Malcolm. He was the 1st of them to talk to me...he was like "can i have <u>your</u> #?". He's like friggin hot and really bad boy. He's gotten in 23 fights and he has a scar under his eye from 1 fight. He's gotten suspended like 5 times, and he has a DSS [[state Department of Social Services]] worker. He also smokes mad weed (since he was 11). Too bad for me he lives in [...] ☹. He plays lax [[lacrosse]] too lol. Chester was cool but I think he was really into Audrey. [...]. We went to this kid Myle's house... he was cool and <u>MAD</u> rich but I didn't talk to him that much cuz he only chilled w/ us for like 45 mins. He was like baby cute... Neways I had a good time, I don't even act like I have a boyfriend which is bad but w/e. I'm praying so hard that I'm not pregnant ... that would absolutely ruin my life ☹. OK well I'll ttyl!

    -   Amy

June 18th, 04'

Hey.. kinda shitty day today. First of all, Roy called me and he was like 'hey babe, i wanted to talk to you about summer, i mean we're both not gunna be around very much so do u wanna still like stay together?' n i was just like 'ya… maybe we should break up'. So it's over. Just like that. I'm happy in a way because i'm not being pressured anymore but i just cannot believe this all happened so quickly. I mean I did so much w/ Roy in so little time. He totally used me and that sucks. I told a lot of ppl I dumped him ‾. I am just praying that I'm not pregnant…It's like a 1% chance but still it's so scary to think about… OK i'm freaking myself out thinking about this so i'm gunna stop… oh yeah Wilhelm n i are meeting at the mall tomorrow (maybe). I went to see Harry Potter 3 with Lily and my Dad today… that was pretty fun. OK well I'm gunna go take my vitamins, pray, then go to sleep. G'night ☺.

> ~Amy

June 23rd, 2004

Hey, I'm on the plane going to Hawaii to visit [my dad's friend's] family. It's been so long since I've written but idk i'm just trying to keep my mind off the whole pregnancy thing. Like I've totally convinced myself I'm not… I didn't have sex with him and my discharge hasn't turned any weird colors. I'm just waiting to get my period. If it's not here by July 1st I'm gunna start getting kinda worried, but no earlier cuz I did have it 2ce in May. This is seriously my worst nightmare though… ☹. If nothing ever goes my way for the rest of my life (if I'm not pregnant) I'll be happy. OK so let's get my mind off that… Byron Faenza came over Monday (the 21st). He asked me out and I said yes. I know it's too soon but he's my best friend and I've wanted to date him for a while. I am never having sex again until my senior prom at the absolute earliest, I'm probly just gonna wait till' marriage though… I NEVER EVER want to feel this way again. Hurt. Used. Violated. Extremely regretful. and worst of all, insecure. I don't know what would happen to my future. I just don't know what to do. But, hey, there's still like no chance so I'll be fine… spent good quality time shopping with my mom this week. I'm going to miss her a lot. OK well I gtg… 2 hours till we land.

> Ttyl
> > - Amy

June 28th

Hey!! This is officially the best day of my life! I got my period when I woke up! This is like Oh my gosh… like i'm SO lucky! IM NOT PREGNANT! I haven't written in a long time but that's only because I've been too scared and it like freaked me out so much to think about it. Okay so let's recap everything that's happened since I got here (Hawaii). I went to [our friends'] new apartment right on Waikiki beach, then I came home and met [his daughter and son] who are the nicest kids - - the son is the most adorable kid I've ever met. They really helped me keep my mind off things. Like it would've driven me crazy if I didn't have them to think about instead of my possible pregnancy. OK so anyways. we went on vacation [...] (which was amazing). I spent a lot of time with the eight kids (ages seven to eleven) that were on the trip with us and of course the daughter and son. I had SUCH a bad day on the 26th tho. My mom found the sheet in my recycling bin from my diary that said I was scared of being pregnant. I thought she'd be angry but she was actually very supportive. I told her I was scared cuz he fingered me and I "thought I might get pregnant from that". I couldn't bring myself to tell her what really happened. This has been like the scariest 2 weeks of my life, I have more to write about (Byron, Wilhelm etc.) but I'll do it later cuz I'm gonna go play with the son. Ttyl!

♥ Amy

July 1st, 2004

Hey,

very eventful day today. OK so when I woke up this morning I was dating Wilhelm and Byron. Idk why but I just feel like I need to have more than 1 guy to always be happy. Byron was that 1 guy that I thought I could live with. U know? Like, ugh, ... he was just really good for me. Unfortuanetly we got in a fight today which really pissed me off because it was over the Olivia thing. Byron got mad @ me for not apoligizing to Olivia cuz [her brother is] his best friend n stuff. That really fuckin pisses me off but just because it was Byron I was willing to let it go but he wasn't! He dumped me...i'm actually pretty sad cuz i know we could've had so much... he also said he did it b/c he likes being single during the summer. Oh well ⌣. Ok now for the weird thing. Sally IMs me n shes like "I talked to Roy... he wants to get back together w/ u". I was like hmmm.riiight.... then Roy IMs me and we talk for like an hour n he's all like 'i'm sorry for breakin up w/ u idk y i did it... i still love u' n then he asked me out. I said i needed the nite to think... I just can't believe he wants me back... like wow... idk...

- Amy

July 3rd

Hey sup [[what's up]]? OK so I said yes to Roy. Idk why... I mean I don't like him, I don't see a future with him, and I can't trust myself when I'm with him. I guess there are 2 reasons that I can think of and they are #1 for my self esteem and #2 to look good. I just want the strength to feel good about myself and not need a guy (or 2) to make me feel like I'm worth something… ugh… I just got offline w/ Roy… I like doing stuff with him but i don't like feel a relationship other than physical stuff. Also even if I did want it to work out I'll probly never be able to go to his house cuz my mom knows about how he "fingered" me. I think I might take him to the movies and see how it goes. Then there's Wilhelm. He says he's in love w/ me but I don't think he knows what love is. I don't even know what love is. Every guy just wants play from me. Like I thought some ppl were different like Irving Edam (who I'm seeing in like 2 weeks) but he was like 'darn' cuz I said I wouldn't fuck him. Idk though. I'mma go 2 sleep now – ttylz…

♥ Amy

July 10th

Hey! I know I haven't written… I've just been SO busy… OMG it's July 11th… if Roy & I had stayed together this whole time today would only be our 1 month anniversary. 1 month! That's so crazy…it feels like 3 years. So yea I'm still goin out w/ Roy (don't ask y cuz idk). When I told Lily she was kinda jealos… she was like 'OMG WTF U PUSSY' n idk if she meant to say this… i think she just blurted it out she was like 'now ur gunna be w/ him 24/7 just like last time and ditch me again'. w/e. Ugh there's so much to write idk where to start! OK well I went to Boston with Sally Ecorse on Friday. We went @ like noon and first we went shopping around Fanuel hall…OK i'll admit i was dressed kinda like a slut… a pink miniskirt and my eyeliner lol (me triyina look hot). But ok 3 diff. guys *(taco guy, filene's basement guy, haymarket guy) (like 50 year olds lol) told me I was gorgeous to my face and then me & Sally went to this watch stand and there was this black guy with dreadlocks and a cigarette on his ear (he worked there) and I gave him my number cuz I'm stupid! Sally told me (later) that he had a wedding band on so he was MARRIED! omg like that's just scary… he called me when I was babysitting tonight and left me a msg for me 2 call him… like what a freakin pedifile [[pedophile]]… k so then we did a lil more shoppin then we went to the Sox game…it was so awesome… like we sat next to this really nice lady, and we won 6-0 and stuff but the best part was when Sally recognized these 2 guys cuz they were her friends friends. So neways they were sitting a few rows down in the next section over so Sally n I got up n on the way back she's like 'r u from my town" n the guys like ya n they talked for literally 20 seconds then we went back 2 our seats. So later I went down to take a walk and Sally didn't come so on the way back I was gunna go talk to the guys but one of them (Sergei) actually stopped me to talk!! He was like 'hey, how'd that girl know where I waz [[was]] from' n i was like 'idk lol' then the guy was like 'sit here, the ppl left' so i got my stuff n came down. I talked to them for a while… they smoke trees [[marijuana]] n drink, they just graduated from high school, they work at a boathouse near my Town…etc etc etc… so i was all ready to ask for Sergei's # @ the end but <u>HE ASKED FOR MINE!</u> so i gave it to him and he text messaged me this morning but it was @ like 8:30 AM so when i got it it was too late but i deff. wanna chill w/ him. O yea and on my way outta the sox game there were these guys n they were like 'that one rite there' 'oh that one or the other' 'her rite there' … lol i <u>think</u> they were talkin about me not 100% sure tho… I wish I'd talked to them but I'm stupid! Oh yeah I bought running shoes 2day n went running. cross country prep. I'm trying <u>REALLY</u> hard this year to do well. Idk why I just have this motivation to do it. I'm scared that I'll grow up and look back @ what I did and what I coulda done and totally regret everything. neways – time 4 bed. write more asAp!

♥ Amy

July 11th
Hey…
Went running around the block today, then came home and watched Degrassi. I'm <u>sooo</u> in love with that show OMG! Then I went online for like 4 hours and downloaded 2 lost episodes of Degrassi called Accidents will Happen (parts 1 & 2). Noggin decided not to air these episodes because they were about one of the characters (Manny) getting an abortion. I just don't understand how Noggin could take it off the air. Like so many teenage girls go through it. Its just so scary to think that I could've been in Manny's position. When I was scared of bein every little thing scared me. If I had a stomach ache I'd think 'that must be the baby growing' n like every second felt like minutes cuz I kept thinkin about it. It was the worst feeling in the world…not to know if my life would go 1 way or the other. Whatever. I'm just so grateful that I'm not. I decided I want to be a pediatrist when I grow up. That'd be neat. A foot doctor ☺. Ima [[I am going to]] go - - i'll write asAp.

♥ Amy

July 12th
2:39 AM
I can't sleep. Probly cuz I took a like 5 hour nap today! Also I'm keeping the light on so my fish Mr. Guppy can find his food, cuz he can't see anything

in the dark. […] I hope Lily doesn't want me to sleepover – i'll b way 2 tired. Wilhelm found out that I was dating both him and Roy so he got upset and broke up with me. What a loss! (sarcastic). I know I sound like a total bitch for saying this but I only keep him around for my self esteem… i'll kinda miss the compliments and poems and stuff but oh well. At least I've cut down with the boyfriends to only 1! Roy. I frankly don't know what I'm gunna do about him. This is gunna sound SO shallow but I hafta be honest… the only reason I'd stay with Roy is to have a date to the fall ball… that's not worth it…. UGH. I need to be single rite now. I feel kinda bad for Wilhelm because of what I did but I mean c'mon he was a compulsive liar. I'm a very confused little gal rite now! Arite [[all right]], Ima try to sleep. ttyl.

    ♥ Amy

7/13/04

Hey. Kinda shitty day. Actually really shitty. Wilhelm IMed me and like spazzed about how he rules and how he was fucking with everyone and shit. Whatever. Then Roy was being unflexible and gay about the movies 2mrw. He's all "I can't go till' later, just come over my house" n I asked if his friends mom could drive n he immediately responded 'no … she can't'. I made the decision that I hafta dump him tomorrow. I'm depressed just thinking about it, because it's gunna be the first time since June 1st or somethin (w/ Wilhelm) that I won't have ANYONE. [...] I just do not want to go back into depression. I've been doing so well. I had my 1st oboe lesson today and practiced for at least 2½ hours no joke. I also went for a run and ran around the block in 16:35 (a minute faster then my record). I might try sprinting it tomorrow. Then I prayed w/ my dad (after I went babysitting). If I get depressed my motivation is gone. I'll spend my time feeling bad for myself. I can't let this happen. This is why I can't have a social life if I wanna go to college. Because of shit like this. I've decided not to have a social life. But what if that makes me more depressed? Is it better for something great to fail or for that great thing never to happen? ugh

    -Amy

July 17th 04'

O… MY… Gosh… I have so much to write about its not even fuckin funny… OK so let's start from like 3 days ago… I started talking to Grady and after a lot of talkin we decided to go to the movies with him n his friend Kiefer. So at the time I was still dating Roy K? So I tell Roy n he's like "I can't go" so I'm like 'OK' but then like an hour b4 the movie starts he calls n's like "I can go" so it turned out to be me, roy, this other guy, lily, kiefer, and grady. It was interesting... I mean Roy looked <u>so</u> ugly so I kept trying to ditch him n sit with Kiefer but finally I just took him outside n then back in and we sat on the bench and I was like 'idk if this is gonna work cuz my mom knows that u almost got me pregnant' n blah blah blah but he was like 'no, i broke up with u once i'm not gonna lose you again'.' So I was like 'uh....' n then we went back in the theatre n i sat next to kiefer the whole rest of the movie. Me and Lily kept gettin up to go to the bathroom and the ppl behind us were getting <u>so</u> pissed but neways 1 time we went out these guys started talkin to us and the white guy asked for my (not lily's) # and gave it to the guy in the middle (who in real life is <u>SO</u> fine! I hope they call. Oh yeah the Jamaican married guy [...] called my cell a lot n i found out he smoked trees and stuff. But neways on the way out of the theatre n Roy kept tryin to hug n kiss me but i made up an excuse that i was running from the manager n i went n hid in the girls bathroom. Ya so I told everyone that I dumped Roy. I treated him like shit but he deserves it. So neways Grady called @ like 11:30 last nite n asked if we would hang out w/ him today. We hadda bullshit our rents' so much to go (we said we were going to play basketball). I brought 2 water bottles filled with alcohol and Grady supplied like ½ bottle. We drank but not enough to get drunk (except Kiefer). We played truth or dare and (without going into every little detail) ... Lily and Grady made out (a lot), [...]. Good for Lily. [...]. About time, rite? The bad thing is (i asked like 30,000,000 times to make sure) he doesn't like her and he doesn't wanna go out with her. Me n Kiefer hooked up a lot (he's the best kisser yet – even if he was drunk), and I flashed him (as a dare) and [...] OK so anyways it was fun, and they wanna hang out again sometime really soon but I'm not that much into Kiefer. He told me I was much hotter than Lily but, idk, I was kinda more into Grady. That is until I found out he told Lily I seemed 'easy'. Bastard. He told me that Lily was too 'fuckin prude' for him. Whatever. Skrew him! I don't need him. Stupid Grady... K so when I got home I got online and Roy IMs me n he's like (on a secret s/n [[screen name]]) 'Amy, why'd you block me?' I was like 'This isn't Amy... Amy dumped you' n he was like 'tell her bye - - its over'. Then I was like 'she already dumped u a long time ago'. Ugh. Then I unblocked his main s/n and on his buddy profile it was this rap about what a sucking hobag slut etc. I am. It's <u>so</u> LONG. I'm wicked sad b/c every guy I've gone out with this summer has ended up HATING my guts. I'm also sad grady called me easy. That sucks that I gave off that vibe. And like deep down I know its true. I've said no to like 2 guys in my entire life. I walk around like a little slut so guys will ask for my number. I hate myself. I think my Zoloft is working because I don't have that urge to cut myself like I used to. OK well I'm gunna get to sleep now… night.

AMY

July 18th
9:26 pm

Hey! I'm in the car on the way to my condo for 4 days to chill with my friend Irving from New York. [[Amy met him at summer sleepaway camp]] Dude b4 I forgot - - you know the guys that talked to me and Lily at the movies? The black guy with the yellow jersey just called me n he was like 'hey, i just called to tell you that ur really hot'… I was like OMG SWEET! So I told him that we hafta chill next weekend so he's gunna call me later. OMG he's so sexy! ☺ Anyways I'll write later. cya!

♥ Amy

July 18th
11:36 pm

Hey again… i'm @ my condo… OMG the black guy (from the movies) called me back! We talked for like 8 minutes … I found out his name's Gilbert (hot name), he's 14 (good cuz i kno he won't like use me) n he lives in Canalboro. So Saturday night we're going to see a movie, 'anything i want' he said. He asked if he could kiss me @ the movies which was <u>adorable</u>! I said ya. Then I said I had to go, and I asked him to call tomorrow. He said 'i love u' @ the end! It was <u>sooo</u> sweet! I said it back, even though I don't even kno him. He's adorable. He has diamond earrings - - HOT! Cyaa!
♥Amy

July 20th [2]
12:25 AM

Hey, Irving came today. He's much better looking than the pictures he sent and than he was in 7th grade. We watched TV, then went swimming, then took showers, then went grocery, video, and drug store shopping, then picked up subs for dinner, then came home but the VCR was broken so we went rollerblading in the dark which was fun. We laid down next to each

---

2. Amy is 15 ½.

other and looked at the stars. We tried to sneak out to go night swimming but the light was on at the poolhouse so it looked like someone would catch us if we tried (cuz one of the rules is "no night swimming"). We came back in around 10:30 and watched TV. He tried to kiss me a few times but i pulled away. I don't like him so why kiss him? Unfortunately I popped open a Corona beer so I got all wild... not b/c i was buzzed, but b/c i was psyched to be drinking beer. I ended up makin out w/ him... Idk why... I guess I felt kinda bad cuz he hasn't hooked up forever and he's always being told by girls that they 'just wanna b friends'. Dude, Gilbert called and we talked a little. OMG he told me that Clive (the white guy) was gunna try to steal me away from him... that made me feel special. Then, later i put my phone in my room to charge and I told my mom to tell me if anyone called, but Gilbert & Lily called after 11:30 so my mom answered (w/out me knowing) n yelled at them. I'm so embarrassed!!! I fucking HATE my mom. Ugh. TTYL
—AMY

> July 21st
> 1:20 AM

Hey. Had a rollercoaster of a day today. Irving and I went swimming and these guys that work here came over (cuz i invited them). They're 16, 17, and 18. There's an ugly sheltered fat kid named Herman (16), A good-looking kid named Gomer (17), and a funny as shit kid named Sargeant (18). We talked for ½ an hour on the porch, then we drove up to this mulch pile and talked for a while. They're all party animals (cept' Herman) Gomer decided to throw a party this Saturday but idk if I'm goin cuz i'm supposed to meet up with Gilbert @ the movies on Sat. Neways i would be really into Gomer but he's his bosses daughters boyfriend so that sux. They hadda get back to work so they drove me n Irving back to our condo n on my way in Gomer asked what we were doin for lunch 2mrw and I said nothing so hopefully we'll chill. Later me n Irving went to the mall. Irving went in the food court to get a pepsi, and i went out to see some guys that were smoking. I sat @ a table near them and 1 of them was like 'hey what r u doing' n i was like 'nothing' n we talked for a while and I asked if they knew of any place to get trees. They called a bunch of places and eventually the 2 younger dudes Georgio (ugly) and Valentine (hott) found a guy. I gave em' my $40 and they swore on their lives theyed [[they would]] bring me back weed. They never came back. I'm so FUCKIN pissed. This is the 2nd time this year i've been ripped off on a weed deal. I guess I learned my lesson tho. Irving cheered me up by paying for ½ of a Coach purse lunchbox thingy but i'm still fuckin pissed. Oh well. So tired cya
– Amy

p.s. lots of Gilbert stories 2 tell!

July 21st
6:10 pm

Hey…got kinda sunburnt today. Did lots of swimming. One of the worker guys (Herman) came over and watched a little TV. The hot guy Gomer walked by while i was tanning by the pool and invited me to lunch 2mrw. He said I can bring Irving if I want but we both agreed he's (Irving) really annoying and kind of gay. I'm not tryina be mean but he trys [[tries]] to be around me like every single second and he's always hugging me and stroking my leg n stuff, lol. His breath stinks too and idk… he's really nice and really sweet but just so friggin annoyin. I'm up in my room rite now to get away from him. Neway onto other things… I've got a big schedule this week… 3 more days till I meet up with Gilbert! It sucks that my summers ending soon. I've met so many people! Alrite well I'm gunna go – I'm gunna listen to my iPod then go out for dinner @ 8. Ttyl!

~Amy

July 22nd
5:44 pm

Hey! Irving left (finally). He was getting so annoying. All he wanted to do was make out. I did a couple times but not at all 2day cuz he was pissing me off n following me everywhere! […] I had a lotta fun with the worker boys overall. I'm trying to get my mom to take me and Lily up there from Sunday morning to Tuesday morning OMG tho I have <u>HUGE</u> news. Well its not that huge but it is to me. OK u know those 4 guys that were at the mall the other day that ripped me off on the weed deal? OK well my mom made me get out of the car to return videos and on my way back guess who I saw driving in? Lyle! He's one of the 4 guys (the tall, blonde nice one)! Dude he looked at me when he was driving in and mouthed 'is that you?' I told my mom he was my basketball coaches assistant in 4th grade and then I went over to his car. It turns out He had no idea they ripped me off - - see, when I was talking to the guys on Tuesday Lyle went off to chug the beers in his car so the police wouldn't find them …one of the 4 guys has bulshit w/ Lyle b/c Lyle stole his girl. So neways on his way out, this guy smashed Lyles windshield and made a huge shatter which is gunna cost Lyle $200 to fix! Poor guy! So today when I was talking to him he's like "he took your money & broke my windshield…. motherfucker." I got his cell # n i'm gunna call it tonight. He says he'll hook me up w/ some trees cuz he feels bad. Hopefully I can see him when I come back up to our condo Sunday. Alrite I'm out… ttyl!

♥ Amy

July 23rd
12:29 AM

Hey! OMG so Lyle (the tall blonde guy) and I talked and I found out that Valentine and him are good kids. They were on their way to go get the weed n Georgio was like 'gimme the money i'm gunna go give it to the dealer' n so Valentine handed it to him and he goes 'i'm keepin it'. Lyle was like 'no ur not, we're goin to give it back to the girl rite now' but Georgio punched him in the neck and then punched his windshield so it shattered. Then he got outta the car n Lyle made him walk home. I feel <u>so</u> bad that Lyles windshield got broken over <u>me</u>! N on top of that he was like 'once i pay for my windshield repair i'm gunna get u ur [[your]] money back'. I was like NO u don't have to! I mean c'mon the kid's lost $210 over me i'm not letting him give me $ b/c someone else stole my $. I asked if Valentine did nething bad n he's like "no, when we were walkin outta the food court, i'm not gunna lie to you, i was checking you out n Valentine wanted u as much as i did so we wanted to get the stuff to u... Georgio was the fag who took the $". I'm so flattered! We agreed that we wanna chill soon so I'm going up to his cabin this Monday. I'm wicked exited cuz he's so nice! He's not bringing Valentine because "things looked like they were heatin up between u and valentine, and i want u for me". Very sweet. I just hope I don't get raped! Lol well i'm pretty tired out from this eventful day... I'll ttyl!

♥ Amy

July 23rd
midnight

Heyy! Went to the Sox game and shopping with Lily. We were dressed kinda skimpy, i'll admit but we got so much attention from guys. No joke, like every guy I looked at that i wanted looked back and either smiled, waved, or approached me. First there were these guys from Conneticut at Fanuel Hall. Then there were countless more. These guys in the stands got up and shouted to me and were like 'how u doin!' Then I was goin to my seat to get my stuff and this guy was like "hey 33" (the # on my shirt) and he was like 'wassup' [[what's up]] n then he waved n i waved n then me & Lily started walking down the stairs and the guy goes "wat [[what]] – u leavin? Don't leave!". Then I told him to come so he came out n he was like "hey im Kirk" n all this shit n he asked for my # n i gave it to him. Oh yeah I was bein such a bad girl - - I was like a mirror image of Audrey. I was hiding from behind this random pole and this like 28 year old guy was like "hey baby and he offered to buy me a beer (when I asked). I ran to get Lily tho and when I came back the guy and his friend had left. Then I went up to these like 30 year olds and asked them to buy me beer but they said no (in a nice way tho). We kept talking for like 10 minutes but then Lily came up 2 me n she was like 'there's an official rite there'. So I turn around n theres this fenway official watching us to make sure we didn't get beer. We walked away but he followed us for like 5 mins. When we stopped, he'd stop. When we walked, he walked. Luckily we lost him! On the train ride home these guys were talking about one of us being hot but idk who he was talkin bout. Neways, we got quickly dressed back into our baggy shorts (we wore that in front of my mom and changed to our skirts when she was out of sight). Neways ttyl!

♥ Amy

July 26

Hey waddup? Dude, I still have stuff to write from my date with Gilbert on Saturday but I don't want to forget everything that happened today. First we (Lily + me) went out to visit the worker boys. Then we went swimming. I talked to Lyle on the phone and we agreed to meet up at the mall at 3 then go chill at Lyle's house. I told my mom we were going to go see a presentation on make-up at Claire's from 5:00 – 8:45. She dropped us off and then we met up w/ Lyle outside the GAP. He's not allowed to drive ppl other than his family (by law) so I was scared but it was friggin cool. He called me up to sit in the front and Lily sat in the back. We drove up to his cottage. He was drivin like 60 mph in the 35 zone.. it was wicked scary! It was awesome tho. He told us about how his uncle started givin' him weed & cigarettes at age 8. By 9 he was popping pills and smoking. At 10 he was using lots of shit on a daily basis and he ran away for 2 months @ 10. He knows all the cops in & around the village. Then he asked Lily if she smoked and she said no and he asked if she'd mind if we did and she said 'no, not at all'. So he took out his bowl and I did it. I SMOKED WEED. I've been pretending to smoke and do drugs since like November 2003 and today I actually did it for the first time! I have to say it's not as great as I expected. I didn't know how to do it at first but Lyle explained it to me and I took a couple hits. It kinda burned my throat but you get used to it. We passed <u>3</u> police cars when we were driving so I was

7/27

sry to interrupt my last entry but im really sad. Right before we came home my mom told me that she had some bad news. It turns out when we were at the condo one of our cats got into my room and knocked over Mr. Guppy's fish tank and ate him. I wasn't that sad at first but now its nighttime and I can't stop thinking about him. Its my fault for sure. He used to live in his small tank but have a big tank around the small one so the kitties wouldn't get at him but then he looked so happy when he was just in his tank with no big tank. So I didn't put the big tank back on and now he's dead. I feel so sad because he was always so scared of even me and I just can't even imagine how scared he must have been when it happened. I didn't even get a picture of him. I miss my fishy.

☹

June [July] 28th

Hey… Went to the used book sale today. w/ Audrey. She mite be my BFF @ BVMP rite now. It would be Loralee, but Lora can never do anything. We did a lil shopping @ Staples, the Verizon store, and the mall after and OMG guess who we saw when we were in Target? Wilhelm! He was with this disgusting fat chic…like no joke she was one of the ugliest girls i've ever seen. She was all punk and her hair looked like a rats nest! Audrey was like "what did Wilhelm pull that out of a sewer". LOL! Wilhelm was actually looking quite cute! He had spiked up hair and finally a non gay outfit! I still haven't told Lily I'm not going to RPHS. She's gonna be so sad when i tell. Ugh. Speaking of Lily, she got invited over Gradys house today. I was kinda jealos at first but not after a few minutes. He's using her. He told me he didn't like her @ all… Lol i'm just a jealos bitch. Lets see wat else? Oh yeah I've been talking to Elyssa Nebo (the only sane person in my school) which is a big step cuz i was scared shitless of her last year! Gtg Cya!

♥ Amy

* cont. from July 26

really scared cuz if we got caught we'd be in <u>so</u> much trouble. Anyways, so we got to his house and he dropped us off @ the end of his road (so his mom wouldn't know he was driving us. Then when we were walkin in a car drove by and Valentine was in it (the one from the mall). His car pulled over and he was like 'we'll stop by later'. So anyways me and Lily went into Lyle's house (which is literally less than ½ a mile away from my condo). We watched "the butterfly effect" and Lyle was kinda turned toward me on the bed. Here I'll show you. LoL.

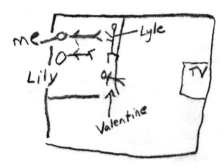

Lookin back on it now, I really wish I would have been more into Lyle at the time - - cuz rite now I really like him. Only problem was, Valentine came by and at the time I thought Valentine was hotter than Lyle, so I was bein all flirty with him... and I tried to sit next to him on the bed instead of Lyle and I kept stealin covers and bein all girly w/ him. Ugh. I was sitting kinda far a way from Lyle so he suggested that Valentine move up next to Lily and Lily move next to me, and me next to Lyle. But I was being too stupid so I pretended not to hear him. Something that really surprised me about Lyle was that he didn't try to make any moves. Not even a kiss. I found that really sweet. He poked my arm 1nce and my leg 1nce (in a flirty way) but that's <u>it</u>!

[…] Anyways, later Lyle was like 'guys wanna go outside and smoke?" and (naturally) I was like hell ya! So we told his mom we were gunna walk up to the village High School. We went across the street onto this little pathway thing and into the woods. Lyle n Valentine lit up 1 bowl and rolled 1 joint. I took quite a few hits! […] Valentine was high for sure. His eyes were droopy n he was all like "yaaah mannnn". […] I didn't feel it but Audrey told me (later) that you have to want to be high, and you have to relax for it to kick in. Oh yah I did call Audrey from the woods so she'd know I was smokin and not lyin about it! When we smoked everything, we walked back up to the village High School to meet Lyle's grandma. We went n played b-ball n then Lyle's Grandma picked us up and dropped us at the mall. When we got there we smelt so much like weed but all the stores were closed! We thought they closed @ 10 but it was 9! We called my mom to tell her to pick us up and then we snuck into the food court bathroom and splashed ourselves w/ water (we didn't have any perfume). My mom came n didn't notice at all! We totally got away with it! Even if we had gotten caught – it'd still be worth it! Looking back on it, I'm happy I did weed. It's not gunna be an addiction but at least I can say I did it w/out lying. Also, now I won't be <u>so</u> obsessed w/ drugs b/c I've tried em' so I know how they r now! Arite well I'll cya!

♥ Amy

Friday, August 7th, 2004

Hey… it's 4:04 AM. I can't sleep @ all… I have so much to write.. Let's see… OK so Monday I went to 9 o'clock mass and had Lily over after for Mister Guppy's funeral. See the thing is: my whole family went to this party thing two hours away, but I wanted to stay home. I cleaned my room like the whole day, and near the end of my vacumming I came across Mr. Guppy's body. It was all crusty and dry. He looked so sad, and scared. When my fam. got home my mom put him in a box and we buried him. Monday morning. I wasn't too pleased with Lily's behavior…she was kind of giggly the whole time…she wouldn't take it seriously.[…] We all wrote messages on the box he was in. I will never forget what my mom wrote. "you were a great fish. I'm so sorry". I love my mom. She cried when we were saying the prayer for him.

After the funeral Lily and I hung out in my room for a while and played neopets. It was fun - - I'm now obsessed. Wat else? Oh yea - - I've been talking to Elyssa Nebo a lot online lately. She keeps tellin me we hafta chill, and smoke together soon. At least I don't hafta lie about doin drugs anymore cuz now i have done weed. I'm so glad I talk to her - - she's really nice. Anyways, i'm wicked tired so i'm gunna go to sleep. Nite!

August 8th

Hey… I think I'm an insomniac. I went to bed @ 4:30 yesterday (AM) and woke up at 10 and tonite I can't get to sleep. I keep thinking about Lyle. He hasn't called since me & Lily met up with him. Idk if he's mad cuz I was flirtin w/ Valentine but I miss him. I'm at our condo rite now. Arite I'm gunna sleep.

cya ☺

~ Amy

August
10th

Heyy… OK I know I haven't written for like <u>EVER</u>. But that's only b/c I've had so much to write and I can never find enough time to write it all! OK so just to clarify stuff from way-back-when - - on Saturday the 24th (of July) I went to the movies w/ Lily, Gilbert, and Clive. Before the movies I was like obsessed w/ Gilbert. Like I'd get so excited wenever [[whenever]] he text-messaged me or called or whatever… Afterwards, I wasn't so into him. Like during the movie (catwoman) all Gilbert wanted to do was make out. It was his first time doing ANYTHING and he wasn't such a great kisser. His tongue went everywhere, and there was so much saliva – ugh! Anyways, we went to 2nd, and sloppy 2nd and he kept friggin grabbin my ass - - it was so annoyin! We got Lily and Clive to kiss 1nce which was cute - - but when I asked him he said he didn't want to go any further w/ her lol. [...] I text messaged Gilbert to see if he thought we were goin out, and he said ya… so apparently now I'm goin out w/ him. He seriously WILL NOT stop calling me and texting me. He's gotten really innapropriate. He's all like 'I wanna hear you moan' and 'r we ever gunna have sex' n stuff. Whatever, I haven't made out w/ne1 since him cuz I don't wanna be like the town slut. I'm goin prude! ☺ ! I'm goin academic too - - like I've been spendin so much time readin (for summer reading) and practicing oboe. I'm very determined to get into a good college. I'll do whatever it takes! Oh yeah by the way I'm at our condo rite now for the week. My brother drove me up here on Saturday (my parents, my sister, and the cats went in the van). My brother and I talked the whole 2-hour ride up. I can relate to him a lot. He left today (Tuesday) cuz he has to go back home and work. Another person I've gotten really close to this summer is mom. I've been a lot nicer b/c she's just an amazing woman and she takes so much shit from all us kids. And I know we're really bonding b/c the other day we were drivin home from the grocery store and she goes "I never woulda [[would have]] believed someone if they told me @ the beginning of the summer that you were gonna be my best buddy - - but it happened". ☺. I love her. Oh yeah, we were at the pool the other day and she told me what happened to her last Friday. […] Poor mom ☹. I feel bad for her. [...] Yesterday me & mom were watchin a movie - - '13 going on 30' and the girl was scared of a thunderstorm so she went to her parents room and slept next to her mom in bed. My mom started crying at that part. She tried to hide it but there were waterfalls rolling down her cheeks. I really don't think it was the movie she was cryin over though. It was b/c she could never cuddle up w/ her mom. Her mom has never even told her she loves her. ☹. I decided that for mom's birthday this year I'm gunna try to get everyone to come down from her hometown. I'm gunna throw a surprise party for Mom. ⊞ Let's see, wat else… oh I told Lily that I wasn't coming to RPHS. She took it better than I expected. I thought she'd cry and be really pissed n stuff…but she's tryin to look on the bright side…She's like "you can live @ my house and sneak to RPHS every day". And she's seriously NOT KIDDING. I hope she'll be arite! God bless her ♥. I talked to Vernon Quemoy online today. I think I might like really like him. Idk why, like I think it's because he's such a sweetie. I know he'd never break my heart or cheat + who knows - - if we went OUT we could end up marrying! He's also like so outgoing and fun to be with. I love him. Another cool kid is Herman. He's the mower kid. He comes over like 3 times a day on his breaks. I'm pretty sure he likes me. He's so nervous around me and he's like jittery and stuff. He's a tiny bit chubby with a black buzz-cut and he's growing a beard rite now. He's not attractive but he's really really nice. Almost too nice! He takes too much shit from people. Oh yeah, Gomer and Sargeant invited me to dinner tonight rite in front of my mom. She didn't object so I assumed it was OK. I got all ready and pretty n stuff n then my mom said I couldn't go! I was like ummm…OK! I wasn't too sad though cuz I didn't wanna go THAT bad. I got some reading and practicing done so that was good. I realized that I can't have a social and an academic life. They both take up so much time. Time that I don't have. I'm gunna have to choose 1. I want good academics cuz i want a good career and life when I'm older, but if I work my ass off my whole life how am i ever gunna enjoy it? As much as I'm told I can have friends and good grades, I'm convinced that that's poo. Total poo. OK well I'm gonna go to sleep. Nighty Nite!

~ Amy

August 11ᵗʰ

Waddup, Waddup? Lol, sry, that's just wat Lyle (his full name is Lyle Okayama) (from the village) says when he's saying hi. Pretty eventful day today. Woke up, went to this bakery […] to get breakfast, then Herman came knockin at my door around 11:40 and invited me to lunch (w/ him, Sargeant, and Gomer). My dad said yes but I wasn't hungry so I told Herman I'd go tomorrow. Oh yeah Lyle O called me back (I left him a voicemail). He told me how this guy stole an onze [[ounce]] and a half, $200, his pipe, his pouch, and other shit from him. Poor Lyle! He also asked me if I wanted to hang out today. I was like 'ya sure'. I wasn't actually gunna do it but I went for a swim, then took a shower and before I knew it I was putting on my rollerblades to go to his house! It could not have been more perfect. My dad and sister were out and my mom was taking a nap. I told her I was goin out to rollerblade and I'd be back later. When I was going down the driveway, I saw Sargeant storming outta the workers office. I was like 'hey!' and he told me how he got in a fist fite [[fight]] w/ his boss. A FIST FITE. Like omg! Then his boss came out (wen we were talking n he was like 'Sargeant beat it!' So i'm not sure if Sargeant's gunna be coming back. Aww, that'd suck. He's so cool! Ok so anyways I rollerbladed down to Lyles house and when I got there he was waitin for me outside. What a sweetie! We went in and chilled on his bed for a little. I met his friend who's kinda football-player lookin. Not that attractive. A big tall guy w/ a blonde beard n' hair. Lyle n I just kinda sat there - - he had his arm around me, we took pix of us, and we watched Mr. football play Playstation2. Lyle tickled me a lot, but never tried to make a move (even tho I know he was totally trying to look up my skirt!). I had to get back home after like 15/20 mins. of bein there. Lyle gave me a huge hug 😁 then I left. I told my mom i met a girl named Velma (who's really Lyle's lil' sister) and I was all like 'I'm so happy to have a friend that's a girl!' It's perfect cuz now I can just be like "I'm goina [[going to]] Velmas" whenever I go to Lyle's! OK well Imma get to bed now. I'll ttyl!

August 12th

Howdy! My day today was pretty low key. I woke up around 11. I was supposed to go out to lunch with the boys, but it was pouring at 11 so everyone but Herman went home. Mom, my sister and me went to the village center to get breakfast and we rented 2 more movies. Then my sister and Dad went out to an art museum and then to a play so Mom and I had practically the whole day to ourselves. Herman came over for a little and we watched TV and talked. I looked like total shit but who cares? lol. Then he left and my mom read 'secret life of bees' (my summer reading book) to me while i sorted my sister's beads. Herman came back from 3 – 4:30 and we watched this movie called Gremlins on channel 3. He left, Mom and I read some more, and then I cleaned the house. I'm glad cuz I finished my 1st summer reading book before Audrey came (she's getting in 2mrw at 11). In a way I'm scared about her comin. I love her to pieces but I don't wanna get caught smokin or drinkin (which we'll deff. do). It's gunna be my first sleepover w/ Audrey. 2 nights 2½ days. Half of me can't wait for her to come so I can blow off some steam, but the other half senses somethin bad mite happen…oh I tried 2 break up w/ Gilbert today. I was all like "we should just be friends…i'm not ready for sex…blah blah blah…" but then he calls n's like "its ok if u don't wanna but let's just keep going out!" Ah. Annoyin kid. I'm kinda gettin sick of Lily. Like she's totally copying my style. I bought AE jeans on Monday and then she just ordered some. Wat is that? And like all the clothes I started wearing to be more original she's now starting to copy. Whateva [[whatever]] ooo the other day at the mall my mom bought me a [...] shirt from Polo, 3 GAP tank tops, and a shirt from the GAP. I told her it was for school so she didn't take $ outta my clothing budget for it. I'm gonna go to the mall with Audrey tomorrow hopefully. I LOVE shoppin! OK well I better get to sleep. I guess I'll talk to you tomorro!

~ Amy

Hey. i'm so stoned rite now. I'll tell you about my day later. We saw a girl that looked like a gramma. And never forget Audreys 2 diff. color eyes and me running from the car - - my mom's arm! Write 2mrw.

    - Amy Luvin

Waddup Dawg?! Wow… I have so much to write. I had probly the best weekend of my entire life this weekend. Audrey came Friday morning at 11:30. We showed her around the house and then me and her started getting ready for the mall. I was changing and all I had on was my bikini (top + bottom) and Audrey was like 'wow i hate you…you have the perfect body. you're skinny but you have boobs!'. That made me feel good about myself. OK so then we got dropped off @ the mall and Audrey really wanted a cigarette (after shopping for like an hour) so we went up to these kids and Audrey got her cigg. Then we were like 'do u guys smoke trees' n they were like 'ya' and so we went to their car and smoked a few bowls. Oh yeah by the way their names are Rico (but every1 calls him Ship) and Art. Art was kinda fat, but really nice cuz he gave us lots of weed. So anyways we had to go so I bought $5 worth of weed from Art and then we left. I wasn't feelin the weed at first but then it kicked in. I kept trippin over shit and everything was funny. I thought I saw my mom so I started running as fast as I could (cuz I wasn't s'posed [[supposed]] to be wearing a skirt) but it turned out it wasn't her, haha! OK so then we went back to my condo (me and Audrey) and started watchin the movie Clueless. It was gettin pretty boring so we told my parents we were gunna take a hike around the mountain (even though it was pitch black and raining lol). Audrey kept throwin up when we were outside. I think its b/c of the ciggs. but I'm not sure. So then we had Lyle come to my condo parking lot to chill. When he came it wasn't just him it was this ugly kid and another pretty hot kid.. They were just finishing up a joint of chronic (weed mixed with cocaine) … Audrey took a hit but I didn't get any and they never rolled another one! (which pist me off!). The ugly kid and Lyle needed to meet up with this dealer guy so they could get heroin so they took us with them… I didn't wanna go AT ALL, but I was hopin to get more chronic on the road so I went. The first like half hour of the ride I was so fucking scared that ~~my parents~~ the police were gonna fuckin get us. Idk wat it was but after a while I was totally calm… I didn't care if the po's [[police]] got us. I was so relaxed. Weird, huh? We hadda get home so they dropped us off before they did their heroin deal. Rite before we left I called up Katarina's cell phone and left a message of the car music blasting and all of us talking. Idk why I did that … maybe to prove to her I have friends and I do drugs. lol. Idk. It was set up so it looks like i called by accident (which is awesome). Oh yeah durin the ride Audrey gave me her weed cuz she didn't wanna be caught by the po's. When we got out of the car I told her I gave it to Lyle and I kept it for myself HAHA! So anyways we got back home and (once my parents went to sleep) we called up Ship and Art and had them drive up to my condo. They parked across the street so we went and sat in their car facing my house (so if any lights went on we could run in). We smoked a few bowls and each drank a bottle of Mike's hard lemonade. Then Audrey bought 2 grams of Art's weed for $30. After like an hour, we decided to go in. We gave Art and Ship hugs … and Ship kissed me on the cheek! I don't know for sure but it kinda seemed like he was into me. Anyways, we (me + Audrey) went back inside and watched 'Half Baked'. We were so fucked up. Haha. Wow. OK so all that shit happened in 1 day. Crazy, huh? Ok so let's continue about the rest of the weekend. Saturday morning me and Audrey woke up and went out into the woods to smoke a bowl. Audrey calls that the wake n' bake haha. Anyways then we went out to the pool (Herman was there) and tanned and went swimming. We called up Ship and Art and had them come swimmin with us for like an hour. Then we had my mom drive us to the food court cuz we were gunna 'go shopping' then 'get lunch'. We actually ate lunch at the food court then had Ship and Art drove me, Herman, and Audrey out to their campsite. When we pulled up the sexiest guy I've like ever seen came out of his tent. Mario. What can I say about Mario? He's beautiful! […] Audrey and I were both just like drawn to him. We also met this fat 21 year old also named Mario but we called him Bud because we didn't wanna confuse him w/ hot Mario. Me, Audrey, Bud, Art, and Ship drove up to this convinience store and me & Audrey each gave Bud $10 to buy us liquor. He bought a $12 and a $6 bottle and I got the $12 bottle cuz Audrey didn't notice the difference so then we went back to the campsite and me, Art, Audrey, and this other kid smoked some bowls in the tent. Then we went back outside and I got lotsa pics of Mario and sat on his lap for a lil bit. ☺ Then it was time to go home and so Mario gave me and Audrey hugs and he kissed me on the lips!! It was just a peck, but an awesome peck! I made Mario come with us to drive us home and we sat together in the back seat. Bud tried to come but he was too fat so there was no room for him on the ride home. I got Mario's # and then he handed me his phone and was like 'put ur # in there… i already got ur name there' and it said 'sexy' under name!!! Like OMG!! ☺ Mario thinks I'M sexy! Ya anyways I think Ship was mad cuz he kept lookin back out of the corner or his eye. Then he asked Audrey for her #. Arite so anyways they dropped us off in the village center and my Dad got us. When we got home we went out to Indian food then when we got home we called Lyle and he said he could pick us up whenever so we told my mom we were gunna go 'play basketball w/ Velma'. Only problem was she insisted on driving us because I don't think she believed that's where we were really going. We had Lyle send out Velma to meet my mom and bullshit for us. She's actually wicked cool. She acts like she's 15/16. We chilled w/ her for a lil bit then Lyle and Valentine came to pick us up. We drove around and smoked chronic n then headed over to Valentine's Dad's house. I was so wicked high. Valentines dog barked and Audrey was like 'shit' and it was the funniest thing in the world! I could not stop laughing. We were hangin out in this little cabin thing and Valentine's dad saw me passin the bowl and he comes over and he's like 'wheres the bowl? I don't want you smokin if I can't have some' !!!!! Then he took a hit out of the bowl! He's seriously the coolest dad I've ever met. Anyhoo… Valentine got a call from his mom and she wanted to come over there to make sure Lyle wasn't there cuz he's not allowed to be near Valentine (cuz she hates Lyle). Lyle wanted to bolt but we were like 'no let's stay' so he just parked in the back yard. Anyways Valentine gave us some free chronic (🌿) then we went back to Lyles car. We waited there for like 30/40 mins in the dark, making no noise cuz if Valentines Mom found us… I can't even begin to explain how screwed we'd be. I was getting so scared cuz it was already 10 and we weren't home. Finally, at like 10:08 Valentine ran out and he was like "okay u guys can leave now - - my mom's gone". It was like perfect timing cuz if we left a minute later we wouldn't have been back by 10:15. Arite so we got in and got changed and stuff (Lyle gave me his shirt)! OK so then later me n Audrey just kinda hung out and watched movies and I remembered I told Ship and MARIO to come up to my condo at 11. We called them up and they were already here! My parents weren't asleep yet and the boys didn't have weed anyways so we told them to come sneak into my house at 11. They did - - I pulled out the sofa bed and we layed down Ship – Audrey – Me – Mario. Me and Mario were just sorta cuddling (watchin How High) and then Ship was like 'Audrey I'm interested in you' n Audrey was like 'I'm seeing someone sorry' (even though she isn't seeing ne1). Then Ship was all sad so he went out to sleep in the car. Audrey went to sit on the other couch and call her friend Kenneth. Me and Mario made out a few times … he is the best kisser in the whole entire fucking world. […] He was awesome cuz he coulda tried so many moves on me but he didn't. He put his hand down my pants for like 2 seconds but he didn't finger me or anything. I went on top of him for a while and we did this thing where we both tensed up our legs at the same time. It felt good and it was kinky (don't worry we had our clothes on the whole time!). And Mario totally got me wet. OMG he's so amazingly sexy! Neways - - I told Mario I was tired so he left … then me n Audrey drank some more … I was totally feelin the effects of the liquor… I was so dizzy and I couldn't steady myself. We cleaned up the room and the kitchen and stuff… then we went to sleep. We didn't really do much on Sunday . We woke up around 11 … Audrey smoked a cigarette n I told her its ok if she does weed but she has to quit ciggarettes. I for one will never smoke cigarettes. Weed is something I'll grow out of. I don't even like it that much, I just do it to be cool. If I started cigarettes I could probly never get off them… so I ain't doin them! On yea Audrey found my bottle of Yeger and she was all pissed cuz it was bigger than her bottle. She's all like "I can't trust u". But its all good - - we're cool now. Herman came over to say goodbye … and then we packed up n left. It was overall an amazing weekend. I'm not proud of myself for smoking so much weed… but at least now I know it's not always worth it to sneak out for weed. I could've gotten caught any 1 of those times by my parents (or worse) the police. I think this weekend was all I needed to start doin well in school… because now I've had my fun, and I don't have to worry about proving to anyone that I do drugs (cuz Audrey thought I was lyin about it last yr). Well I'm gunna go now… long diary entry huh?? Haha. Ttyl!

  ♥ Amy

Hey… went over to Lily's tonite. She's gotten really depressed lately. She told me a story that she went over Grady's house one nite and she didn't tell me b4 cause she was embaressed. […] I feel really bad for her… like she's never had a boyfriend and Grady's obviously just using her. She's not in good shape. She doesn't laugh that much anymore and she's just so dull. I stayed till' 9 and then they gave me the fish they got me and I went home. Nothin much else happened … I talked to Sergei online (Sergei from Sally's town…the one me n Sally met at the Sox game). He was all like "we should chill, do u have a boyfriend" n when i said no he was like "y not - - u should have no trouble gettin guys". That was sweet of him!! Turns out he has a g/f but he 'doesn't think that will be lasting that much longer'. OK well imma go watch TV… ttyl!

  ♥ Amy

Hey … wow I've been bad…wow…Let's see 2day I went to […] with my sister and her friend. I bought a bunch of cool stuff and I was gunna go chill with Malcolm but then we hadda go home so I did a raincheck w/ him. I wore a tank top and jeans (cuz I didn't wanna look like a slut) but this like 60 yr old guy told me I had beautiful eyes when I walked by. […] It's cool - - I actually grew boobs this summer so I wore a tank top with no padding, bra (except for the built in bra), or bikini top or anything! Havin boobs makes me sooooo much more secure! […]

~Amy

Hey - - went to the mall w/ Lily 2day. We both wore skirts and tank tops (again w/ no padding) ☺. Lots of guys were checkin us out and these cute guys out-side Aeropostale were trying to strike up a conversation w/ me but I kinda just brushed them off like I was too cool. I refuse to be easy even if its just w/ talking, haha! Neways on the way out we passed these like 18 yr old guys n they were like 'sup sluts?' SLUTS! Excuuuuse me! We were both like almost in tears. That was so mean! We both vowed never to wear skirts again but idk how long thats gunna last! Then I had oboe later and I saw Ophelia Ealing from my car and unintentionally gave her a dirty look. K well I'm gunna go - - I'll see ya!

s/Amy

Hey… not much happened earlier 2day. I went to the dentist, then the psy-chiatrists. Audrey died her hair red and we talked about having a sleepover tonite but then somethin bad happened. She calls me up around 8:30 and she's like "hey Amy - - you can't sleep over cuz I got kicked outta my house" ………. o …. m …… g …. like wow. she said her dad flipped out about her hair bein red and said this was the last straw (he already knows she smokes pot and drinks). He said she either had to shape up her attitude or get out. So she got out. […] Her dad says he's not paying for her BVMP tuition but I hope he changes his mind cuz I'll die w/out her there. I just feel so bad for that family. […] I feel wicked bad for Audrey. No wonder she's so depressed. I can't blame her for smoking cigarettes. OK well I'll ttyl. Pray for Audrey!

~Amy

August 31st
Heyy… lots has happened but I'm not gunna write it all in detail. I talked to Niko and sent him a pic of me but he ended up being a bastard and shov-ing it all in my face by sending the convo to Hilary A and Maeve who sent

it to Lily who wants to tell me all the shit he said to them about me but I didn't wanna hear it. I yelled @ niko and now I don't talk to him nemore. I slept over Audreys one nite and we totally smoked a bowl in her closet! Then again in the morning before cross country. Oh yeah i'm doing cross country. It's actually really fun - - I like it a lot. I actually have a sense of responsibility now which is good. Me n Lily went over Grady's last nite and met his friend Julian who's actually pretty attractive. [...]. We also all smoked a bowl in Grady's closet! Julian thinks Lily's 'pretty good looking' and I'm 'cute' and Lily said he said he's interested in me. I kinda like him...I asked him wat kinda girls he's into and he said cute & outgoing. He said Lily is too much of a friend to go out with. Ahh I mite like him! We didn't do anything...like not even a hug! But he's totally cute n he lives in the next town over. OK well the first day of school's 2mrw so Imma head 2 bed...I'll write a reflection of my summer 2mrw.

♥ Amy

9/3/04

Hey! Omg I have so much to write its not even funny. I started school on Wednesday. It was actually really good. Elyssa Nebo's bein so nice to me. The first day she was all like 'dude Amy when r we gonna chill n smoke some pot?'. We've been talkin a lil. There's also this new girl Nancy Xingu whos like wicked nice and she apparently smokes pot (but I find that hard to believe cuz she looks so innocent). I'm doin really well w/ my grades b/c that way i'll get into college and get onto my parents good side. My mom says she's neva seen me so determined. Well cya!

- Amy

Hey dude!

Big weekend at the condo. I am like soo pist off @ audrey rite now but i'll get to that later. Julian left me 3 msgs the other day when he was drunk. In one of them he was like 'Amy I can't stop thinkin about u... it's weird'. I'm kinda into him ☺. So anyways me n Audrey went to the village and we were @ the mall and there was this WICKED hot guy working at Nautica and he said "Hey watsup' [[what's up]] to me as I was passing by. I kept eying him n vice versa. Then literally rite when I was about to talk to him guess who pulls up? Lyle! So then he yells out 'Amy!' n I go talk to him a little n then it turns out he knew the guy @ Nautica (Jones). He invited Jones to chill later that nite and Jones said yeah. Then when Lyle left me n Audrey went up to Jones and got his #. He said to call @ 6. So later we told mi parents we were going to Velmas n met up w/ Lyle @ his house. We chilled there for a lil and his friend came over too. I really wanted to see Jones so I kept making Audrey ask Lyle to call him n everyone thought Audrey liked Jones. So neways we went over this like 30 year old guys house and Lyle n his friend gave him $ to go out n buy a 30-pack of beer for them. Then we chilled @ the guys house for a lil and smoked a bowl. Then we drove to Jones's house and rite before we went in I told Lyle that Audrey was into him (cuz she is) and he said he'd hook up w/ her cuz he's 'kinda into her'. Then we went and chilled w/ Jones who wasn't as attractive as I originally thought…but he's still pretty good looking. We went over to Jones's barn n chilled there for a bit. […] Jones kept trying to get me to sit w/ him and stuff but I wouldn't. I think its cuz I was jealos of Audrey n Lyle. […] They dropped us back @ my house n then Lyle got wicked pist @ us later cuz we wouldn't sneak out to see him. He's like 'I needa talk to both of u'. He told me he'd been tryina hook up w/ me forever and rite now Mr. Football and Jones both like me. That like melted my heart cuz I like him too but now I don't even have a chance cuzza [[because of]] fuckin Audrey. N Audrey wouldn't shut up about how much she loved Lyle n stuff. I was so depressed… I wanted to cut myself but I didn't. Audrey n Lyle r so tight now too. I miss having Lyle to myself. Audreys ruining everything.

♥ Amy

9/9

Hey! Today was the best day i've had in awhile. This junior named Sabine is in my math class n yesterday she's like 'do u smoke' cuz sum1 told her i did n we had a big talk and i admitted i do. Turns out she told on Miranda Tihuan for smoking in school but that's cuz Miranda supposedly told on her first. Then today I asked her if she smoked and she's like 'yea!'. She can't remember the last day she hasn't smoked weed! We talked for maybe 10 minutes then we had a quiz and we talked some more after and she wrote me a note sayin we should hang out sometime! She's done cocaine 3 times and she 'loves' it. She's done E once (accident tho cuz someone slipped it in her drink). N she smokes a shitload of pot! She says her parents know but they just don't talk to her about it. I'm seriously like so happy cuz I'm makin friends w/ a JUNIOR! Then I think she told Miranda T and this other junior cuz I saw them talkin rite after math and into lunch and kinda grinning @ me. I can't help but feelin happy! ♥ And I'm also kinda makin friends w/ this new girl named Nancy Xingu. She invited me over 2day but I kinda blew her off cuz I said yah but then we didn't like talk @ all. OMG and I've been talkin to MARIO (from the village)!!! Ahhh! He's so awesome! He's bein a sweetie! I mite invite him up for fall ball. Ttyl!

    ~Amy

9/10

Hey! Had a field trip today to see this play. I sat w/ Audrey on the bus ride there. When we got there me, her n Nancy walked around a lil n then we split up so I could get a drink n when I got back this fat guy was in the seat between me n' Audrey (cuz she invited him). Turns out there were a ton of schools there to see the play. I decided to go across the aisle to sit w/ this other kid who was a skateboarder. He's cute but he's really short for a senior which is a huge turnoff. Anyways as soon as I sat over there all the girls (sophomores and juniors) were staring @ me cuz I was w/ a guy. It wasn't like a mean look … kinda like a 'whoa' look. Like even three of the really popular juniors were starin. Then Sabine came over to sit next to me and the skater guy. The play was delayed 1 hour n 45 mins. so we all 3 talked for a little. The skater guy and this other kid said they thought a lot of girls from our school are hot. Sabine got really pist lol. She's like 'no1's hot from our school. Well except for you, Miranda, and April Aube." I'm glad ppl think I'm pretty cuz last year like no1 did, haha. Oh yea n I asked her if she knew that guy Sergei (who I met @ that sox game) n she said yea! Haha. Oh and Sabine invited me to this tatoo and piercing show this Sunday. Audrey's totally being all nice to me cuz she wants to be friends w/ Sabine n I think she's a bit jealos. I was talkin to her about chillin this Sunday (cuz I forgot about the Sabine invitation) and Sabine was like 'NO, come chill w/ me on Sunday!' Haha. I showed Sabine n this girl April Aube the pics of me n Mario n other ppl (like Galen n Lyle). Sabine was like 'ur so pretty!' n April was like 'yah I know I hate u Amy… I think ur wicked pretty." At least now they know I only go for cute guys (they both thought Mario was hot). I'm like really happy to have upper-classmen friends. It's not like a lesbian thing (lol) I just am happy to finally have friends. Oh yeah speaking of friends I feel so bad for Lily… She's wicked sad. Oh yah Elyssa n I are talkin a lil more and I saw her boyfriend pickin her up (he's like wicked cute! Ok well I'm goin over Audrey's for a sleepover… I'll write 2mrw!

    ♥ Amy

9-11-04

Heyy… slept over Audrey's house last nite. It was kinda borin cuz the guys we were gunna chill with never called Audrey so we couldn't smoke weed @ all. Then this morning we had a cross country meet which I totally sucked at! Aw well! I've been talking to Raul a little. He wants to chill - - I told him to get some shrooms. He's not that hot but he has good weed n he'll give me n Audrey lots for free. K well I'm gunna go blowdry my hair and get ready for oboe and babysitting. Ttyl!

♥ Amy

9-13-04

Hey… Had a <u>long</u> day, but it was pretty good. I realized that rite now I'm happier than I've been in a <u>long</u> time. My relationship w/ my parents is good, everyone at school's being nice (I have friends!), my grades are so far very well, and I have more boys then I could ever wish for! I'm a pretty lucky gal! Let's see… Oh Sabine called me last nite @ like 5 to say she couldn't go to the Boston thing but asked if I wanted her to pick me up so we could chill. I said 'yeah deffinetly' but then she found out I was w/ Audrey and she didn't know if she could take 2 people so she said to call her when I knew what was goin on (but I never did). Then 2day in math she asked if I wanted to go smoke after school n I said yah but then we didn't talk the rest of the day. Oh… Audrey's been pissin me off again. She won't stfu [[shut the fuck up]] about Lyle n how he loves her […] I told her we were going to our condo this weekend but I'm inviting Nancy instead. I'm not talking to Lily rite now either. She's pissing me off so I'm ignoring her calls. OK all imma go. bye.

~ Amy

9/18/04

Hey,

Wow I have so much 2 write again! I had my first full week in school and so far my lowest grade has been a 93. I haven't talked to Mario that much… I always talk about him and all my other men during class and track. Oh I ignored Lily all week starting Sunday nite and going till Thursday nite. I just didn't really have enough time. She […] started IMing all my BVMP friends n bein like 'where's Amy? Why isn't she talking to me? I'm worried!'. Ay yai yai. Oh I do have a lot more friends than last year. I'm wicked outgoing and I'm really nice to a lot of ppl. I don't give out dirty looks anymore. […] Oh, u know Julian (Grady's friend)? Well apparently he likes me… We talked for a lil when me n' Lily weren't talking. He blocked her cuz he's sick of her complaining. Lily ended up telling me cuz he told her and I didn't believe her but then Julian n' I talked online for like 2 hours last nite and he's like 'if i c u then I'm just gunna get more attracted to u than I already am and then i'm gunna get hurt cuz u won't like me back" The funny thing is I never told him 'Oh, don't say that, I will like u back'. Usually I'd just say that but idk I just didn't feel like it. I'm into Julian, he's really attractive and hot… but I don't wanna get involved w/ the 3rd member of the Grady - Kiefer – Julian group cuz they'd all just think i'm a slut. Idk we'll see what happens w/ me I guess.

9-21

Holy fucking shit. Guess what? Me, Audrey and Sabine B. smoked chronic yesterday afternoon and then me and Audrey went to cross country and our team figured out we were high and told coach and the gym teacher. They called my mom and she went through my stuff and found the 2 pipes and 2 grams of weed. Of course we didn't know this so we lied our fuckin assess off in the office. I looked Ms. Dirath [[the Athletic Director]] and my coach straight in the eye and said 'I didn't do it… how could you guys even suggest that?' so its been a pretty bad 24 hours. At first when me n Audrey got dropped off Helena Mead & Lenora Liao were like 'Amy… come here for a sec!' n they looked and immediately knew I was high. They go 'Amy if ur high you mite wanna get some eyedrops… ur eyes are totally glazed'. I hafta admit at first I was kinda excited b/c I wasn't even purposely acting high but people could tell so me n Audrey went inside to get changed into our track uniforms and when I was walking through the 2nd floor I saw Miranda Tihuan and another junior in the bathroom so I went in (cuz Miranda's a huge stoner n I guess I kinda wanted to show off) and I was like 'have you guys seen Audrey Sebha?' n they were like 'no', n I was like 'Oh… .. … …… OK' n then Miranda was like "wait a sec… come here … lemme see ur eyes' n i was like 'NO!' n I shut them so no one could see but they knew n they were like 'you are so high!' n Miranda was like 'its OK…i'm like the biggest pothead…ask anyone…ask the principal…ask the dean'. Then Audrey came in and I went to get my gym bag and when I went back Miranda gave me some eyedrops and then they left. At that point (apart from feeling totally fuckin stoned) I felt so cool. I mean juniors know I'm a stoner. That's so cool. So after we changed we went out to our lockers and Tennise Diamant was like 'dude u guys are so high' and it was fucken hilarious - - Audrey made up this bullshit story about how our eyes were only red b/c I was really upset about something and we'd been crying. It was fuckin hilarious and she totally bought it! Then me & Audrey headed over to the gym and that's where the trouble started. When we got in we went straight to the bathroom and Terry Zipaquira saw my eyes and she was like 'Amy...r u high?'. I gotta admit, I wasn't tryina show it off but I wasn't necissarily tryina hide it. Terry told like everyone from the team and for the next maybe 20 minutes every1 was whispering and staring at us. Before that point I didn't really care if ppl knew. Yea, I smoke marajuana. You only fuckin live once - - why have a life that you don't live? But by then I was starting to tense up and I was trying to act normal but everything was sort of spinning and things in my brain like couldn't connect. It was awesome. Then Terry & Carolina Bucara went and told our team captains (I heard them) and then they went into Ms. Dirath's office for like 5 mins. Then they came back out and told us to do our 2 lap warmup. We were all heading out the door when the other team captain said "could u 2 stay back a sec - - Ms. Dirath wants to talk to you". Audrey and I had gone over many-a-time what to say if our parents 'wanted to talk' and she did exactly as planned. 'About what?' she interrogated w/ a tone like 'I didn't do shit...unless u find evidence'. her pupils got smaller and the light blue in her eyes showed. The captain was like 'i dunno' (even tho that was b/s). Then we went into Ms. Diraths office and her and coach were sitting there looking very serious. Then the questions started. 'Were u smoking? Do you know why rumors are being spread about you 2?' etc. I looked both of them in the eye and said I didn't do it... I'd "never be so stupid" etc. It was awesome bullshit too!

....

Amy also wrote an account of the afternoon on looseleaf paper while she was still at school:

I'm such a fucking piece of shit. I'm in homeroom rite now. it's 4 PM. I just got caught smoking pot. Me, Audrey and — went driving after school. We smoked a couple bowls and then we came back for cross country practice. Everyone was like 'you guys are so stoned' and we were like 'um no..' n then ~~a~~ the people from my track team ~~were~~ told the coach and Dirath ~~we went to~~ on our way out (the captain) was like 'could you 2 stay back a sec? Dirath wants to see you'. we went in and coach and her were sitting on chairs and they were like 'there've been some rumors going around about you two'. I was like 'I know, everyone's talking about us. I'm feeling rejected' n ~~the~~ Dirath was like 'well, do you know what this chit-chat's about?' and we were like 'no, and it's outrageous that you'd ever ask somthing like that'. and they were like 'okay, well I want you to know that I've called your mother down and she's coming down rite now just so we can let her know about our situation'. We went back out and started stretching w/the team and everyone was talking about ~~the~~ us. We were just sitting there and everyone was like staring and this girl was talking about how me n Audrey always talk about drugs and stuff. Then Dirath came out and she goes "Amy, your mother found your pocketbook so... we know you lied" and then she started talking about how we shouldn't do drugs and blah blah blah ~~My~~ Rite now I'm sitting in an empty classroom waiting for my dad to get here so the principal, me, and my parents can all have a meeting. Audrey and her dad just got out of their meeting. She came back and mouthed "we're suspended for the rest of the week" and then took her stuff and told me to call her cell phone when I can I just cannot fucking believe this happened. I'm such a fucking douche. My life was not far from perfect, Now I'm suspended, my good start is going down the shitter, and just omg. this means no Florida, no more internet in my room, no more hanging out w/ Audrey.

Hey. So the transition back to school went pretty smoothly. I missed one big religion test [[because of the suspension]] but I'm not gunna let that bring me down. I've made a lot of progress in my friendship with Sabine. I mentioned I knew this kid Sergei who she knows too and we were all gunna chill and we had no school today (Friday) so last nite I chilled with her and Audrey. Audreys been such a fucking bitch lately. Like shes only nice to me when she wants something. She knows im better friends with Sabine than her so she'll b nice to me just to get Sabine and then she'll like totally ditch me. I'm pretty sure Sabine likes me more tho. Yesterday in school shes like "I don't think audreys gunna b able to sleep over—is that ok?'. Dude like seriously I was so depressed the nite b4 cuz I thought audrey was gunna break up my friendship with Sabine, but I guess not. Ok so I kno I haven't written for like a fuckin long time so im gunna like split it up into sections to tell you everthing.

Thursday after school: Me n audrey went out to sabines car where Miranda Tihuan, Sabine, and this other girl were all waiting. We were gunna drive around and smoke a bowl of audreys weed but then Sabine couldn't find her bowl so Miranda T. got out cuz she hadda go. Miranda's been pretty nice too. It's so sad—Sabine told me that Miranda's kinda chubby under her uniform [...] I feel wicked bad u kno? Arite but back to the story. We dropped the other girl off at the gym and then went to Sabines moms house to get her bowl and then smoked like sooo much. Audrey went and sat up front so I was all alone in the back but its all good! Then we went to Sabines dads house to change and get ready. Then we went over this 20 yr old guys house. We chilled there and smoked and ate lotsa food and then left at like 5:30. We picked up this other kid and smoked a couple bowls with him. Then we went over Audreys friend Kenneths house (whos actually not that bad lookin) and chilled with him for a bit. Sabine and the other kid wanted to go pick up someone else and Sabine like really wanted me to go with them but audrey wanted me to stay with her and it was all confusing and me AND audrey ended up both leaving. Then we picked ip this kinda ugly kid [...]. We drove around for a while then went back to his house to drop him off and pick up Fern. We got her and we were heading over to my friend Charles house when my fucking mom called up @ 8 and shes like 'Amy come home now—ur dads sick'. I was so fuckin scared that they like knew we were high or something but she said it was nothing she just wanted me home. Sabine was like 'ill take u home' and she was like totally trying to get audrey to go home too. Shes like 'audrey can I just bring u home too b/c I don't want too much on my hands and im just wicked stressed' but audrey was like 'no I don't wanna go home.. if I cant stay with u then I hafta stay at kenneths house and I really don't wanna do that' n then sabines like 'well wats kenneths number—can u at least try to see if u can sleep over there?'. like she REALLY wanted audrey out too. Anyways they dropped me off at the end of my street and I went in and everything was fine. I think my mom was testing to see if I was high or not by making me come home early. Now at least she trusts Sabine so I'll b able to go there again but I feel like such a loser b/c shes so fucking overprotective. Audrey and Fern slept over sabines and audrey said it was lots of fun. Im pissed I couldn't stay but theres always other times.

The Mario situation: Oh Jeez wat can I say about mario? I asked him to the fall ball and he said yes!!!! He's driving 2.5 hours down from Connecticut just to see me! It's gunna be awesome. Oh and he always calls me sweetie and baby now! He's so sweet! I sent him my school pic b/c he was like begging me to send a pic but I don't think he liked it very much cuz hes all like 'can u send another one?'. Oh well. Omg tho he sent me these fuckin sexy pics of him… OMG!!!! Like with his shirt off and shit.. like ahhhhhh! How fucking sexy can u get? We talk as much as we can so that's good.

The Julian situation: Julian julian julian. (I'm talking about gradys friend julian, not audreys friend). He and I have been talking A LOT. We talked for like 4 hours the other nite cuz he said he'd stay up till I smoked my weed and went to bed. We deffinetly flirt a lot, but idk if we could ever go out because I hooked up with grady and kiefer and if I hooked up with julian itd b like putting a 'slut' sign across my forehead. I think I do have feelings for him but he goes to [a private school 2 towns away] and I go to BVMP and we'd never see each other. Whatever, I guess we'll see wat happens.

The Lily Situation: We haven't been talking at all. Its more of a pride thing rite now. I wont call her because then id b losing the battle. She wont call me because that's a blow to her pride. Its so fucking stupid. I called her today and we talked for a little bit but its not the same anymore. It's all about competition. Every word we say to each other is something that we know will either hurt the other one or make them jealos. I'm not missing Lily that much but I just kinda wish we were a little closer.

I just fucking hate our society. I wanna go off to an island and never have to worry about this shit. I don't even know at im worrying about. Lol. C'est la vi. Lets think happy things. I have a ton of money in my bank account rite now. I have like $500 in there, then $120 in cash and $140 in allowance and then I'll be getting my clothing budget soon. Idk what im gunna buy. See I want to buy a TV or something, but I'll be getting my permit in January and I know my whole entire fucking world is gunna change when I get a car. I won't have to rely on my parents to drive me everywhere. I'll be able to go out and lie about where I'm going. I'll be spending absolutely no time at home. I might wanna spend my money on a new stereo system for the car or something but idk we'll see. Ok well I'm gunna go now because my dad keeps coming in to see what im doing. Ill write a.s.a.p.

~Amy

October 10, 2004

Hey mann.. wats up? Ahh I kno I haven't written in like forever and im wicked wicked sorry but im just gunna cut to the chase cuz I have SO much to fuckin write.. this week in school was ok… we got our progress reports on Tuesday and I got an A, a couple C's, a D and an F. It really pisses me off because if I hadn't gotten suspended I woulda gotten straight A's. fuck this. Oh Audrey and Nancy have started to get really close. Like we'll all be walking together and then they'll go off and walk ahead of me. It was really making me jealos and pissy earlier in the week, but I talked with Nancy about Audrey in study and it turns out Audrey totally ripped Nancy off on this weed deal. Sucks for her, lol.

OMG ok dude-on Tuesday I had to go back to cross country practice but Audrey decided to quit cross country so I had to go all alone. We did our run and everyone was being really nice and friendly but then at the end coach was like 'ok everyone go over there except for Amy. I wanna have a word with you'. I was just like oh shit. I gotta admit I kinda like the attention because everyones like so curious.. u kno? Neways coach was like 'do u have something to say to me?' n I was like 'yea im really sorry and blah blah blah…'. Then he was all like 'u should have said sorry earlier—that's very disrespectful' and shit like that. Then he made me apologize to the whole team!!! It was embarrassing but I did it and everyone was like 'its ok we don't care!'. Audrey decided to rejoin track team the next day and coach made her do the same thing. We were practicing wat she was gunna say and we were thinking about saying 'ok im sorry that you guys felt the need to tell on us.. I guess we forgive you' lol. That woulda been funny. Audrey actually said that to Terry Zipaquira (one of the girls that told the captain on us) but she didn't really take it as a joke haha.

My friendship with Lily is pretty much over.. I hate to say it but its true. We had CCD on Sunday which brought back a lot of memories but we're in like

2 separate worlds now. Our whole friendship is about competition. Her new friend is Juliette Efate and mine's Audrey. It kinda depresses me because if our friendship is discontinued that means theres never any hope for anyone because we were the best of friends. I guess we'll just see wat happens. [...] I went to the mall with Audrey on Friday (cuz it was her birthday) and [...] we went to the LoveSac and saw this really nice guy that works there and chilled there for like an hour (cuz all the stores close at 9:30). We were supposed to hang out with Kenneth (audrey's friend/possible lover) but he hadn't figured out his plans yet so we had the LoveSac dude drive us around in his 2 seater for a while. Lemme tell ya—it was so fucking awesome in there. Me n audrey sat in a seat together and he drove like seriously 95mph in the empty mall parking lot. It was so fucking scary but we got this like adrenaline rush so that was cool. We ended up having him drive us to Kenneth's house cuz Kenneth said he could get us some coke but his dealer was being all gay and wouldn't sell it that late. We smoked a couple bowls of Kenneth's weed and then had Mr. LoveSac drive us back to Audreys house (around 12:30). We said we were at Roller Kingdom with Rosanne Ubangi. Overall I guess Friday was okay.. I felt wicked bad because my mom and I were gunna watch the debates together and stuff (b/c she left to run her marathon Saturday morning). I thought I was gunna have a little more fun at Audreys but hey, what can I do about it now? Saturday made up for it anyways. Me and Audrey woke up around 9 and I decided I wanted to clean her room so we did that for like an hour. My mom dropped by at like 10 to say goodbye. I told Audrey that I wanted to be home by 1 because I needed to start my homework and stuff. That was pretty much ok until Kenneth called and said he wanted to meet up with us at Audrey's ex boyfriend's house, the one she was once seriously so in love with. He dumped her like 3 times, and she can not get over him. He got a girl pregnant and they're having their baby next month. She pretends she's okay but he's seriously like ruined her self confidence and happiness. She always talks about how he's so hot and I really wanted to see for myself so I agreed to walk down to his house with her. We told her mom we were going into town to buy some pizza. When we were walking, Kenneth got out of a car that was driving by and came to walk with us to the ex's. When we got there, the ex was sitting in this broken down car. Me and Audrey each bought an 8th off him for $25 each (which is like scarily cheap). He's cute—but actually a little bit chubby. His mannerisms are wicked sexy though. Like he put a blunt [[a hollowed out cigar filled with marijuana]] out on his tongue! We chilled there for like an hour and a half and then left. We walked down to the pizza place and

had Audrey's mom pick us up there. They dropped me off at home around 4. When I got in, Kalli (my babysitter) called to say that her friend was really upset, cuz her husband left her, and she needed her support. She wanted me to come to her friends house with her so I wouldn't be alone. I didn't want one piece of that, so I talked to my mom and she said I could stay home alone for the nite!!!!!!!!!!!!!!! I was like omg!!! I called Audrey and she decided she wanted to sleep over. I went to baby-sit around 6 and the parents said it was okay for Audrey to come there later. Audrey showed up around 7 and we chilled with the kids and then put them to bed at like 8:30. Kenneth called me and said he had coke and he was willing to sell it for $50 a gram. He was gunna meet us at my house at like 10. The parents came back at like 10 and drove me and Audrey back to my house. When we pulled onto my street, there was a car on the side of the road and Audrey and I immediately knew it was Kenneth. The mom was like "do you know those people" n I was like "no". Then when were pulling into my driveway, KENNETH WAS WALKING OUT!!!! The mom was like 'who are u' n he was like 'I'm lost—where's Railton?'. It was unbelievable, the mom actually bought it. She dropped us off and we went inside. We were like 'holy shit I can't believe that just fucking happened.' Kenneth dropped by when the mom left and I bought 2 grams of coke off him. He left and then me and Audrey smoked a blunt of her ex's weed mixed with my coke ON MY ROOF! Haha. It was fun. [...] Sunday morning I had Audrey's mom pick her up at 10 am (because my mom didn't know she slept over and I didn't want Kalli to tell on us). Me and Audrey wanted to go to the mall later and Kalli still hadn't come so Audreys mom picked me up and we had Kalli meet us at the mall. [...] I bought a lip gloss and a bra (I moved up to a 34C☺) and then Kalli took me out to dinner. We talked a little but – she's like wicked cool. [...] My mom came home Monday afternoon, so I didn't do very much on Monday. It was a cool weekend though. Ttyl!

~Amy

Nov 10th
Wow it's been a while can't go into detail but basically
1)   [...] left school like 3 weeks ago to get homeschooled. Last nite she told me its cuz her boyf got her pregnant, but they ended up having a miscarriage so that's over with. I kinda miss her, but hopefully we'll keep in touch.
2)   I got my belly button pierced! Audrey and I found this girl who does piercings for under-age kids. Audrey got her tongue AND her belly, but I just got my belly. My mom hasn't found out yet and it's been 2 weeks ☺.

3)   Audrey got her stash taken away. Yup. Her dad found her stash in her closet last week (consisting of like 2 grams of weed and some lighters). She admitted to her dad that she does smoke and that she's not gunna stop. He flushed it all down the toilet which sucks for Audrey, but she didn't get in any trouble.

4)   I'm kind of over drugs. you heard me. see, it's just like what happened when I used to cut myself. I loved it when it was a secret, but once I got caught I don't see the fun in it anymore. Like a couple weeks ago me & Audrey were smoking out of a pen on my roof and I was just like 'what am I doing?' I mean before I tried weed I thought it'd be so awesome, but it turns out that weed (along w/ coke) isn't that great. Honestly, the only reason I'm doin it is to impress ppl.

-Nov 28th

5)   over the past month I've snorted coke w/ Sabine and Miranda Tihuan in the bathroom twice (durin lunch). They're both like wicked nice. Sabine invited me to hang out w/ her like every day but i never could cuzza cross country.

6)   I got Lyle back... 2 weekends ago me and my parents went to our condo and (w/ help from Lyle's mom and his sister) I got my parents to let me sleep over "Velma"s house... me n Lyle kinda had that flirty thing goin on throughout the nite but I wasn't sure it was goin anywhere. Oh yeah - - Lyles friend was over and he's really ugly (a lil chubby w/ longish hair) but he's like the coolest kid I've EVER met. Me, Lyle, "Chubby", a guy that dropped by later and his cousin went into Lyle's garage and smoked like 5-10 bowls of mad good weed. I remember the chubby guy putting his jacket on me (this like long trench coat) and then lookin at me n' sayin 'I love marijuana'. Ah! He's so cool! And then later we went in and there were 3 slices of pizza left in the box and i had the munchies so I took a slice of cheese. Then when we got into Lyles room I really wanted another slice. I was like begging "chubby" to get it for me n he was like 'NO' n I was like 'why?' n he goes "B/C if i go out there i'll be tempted to eat the last piece"...Lol! "Chubby" apparently took a pepperoni before...LOL! I guess you hadda b there ... K so then later i was just sitting on lyles bed playing w/ his little kitten (like 3 weeks old) and Lyle came and sat on the other side of the cat. We (me, Lyle n "Chubby") were all just kinda talking n watchn TV. I was like scratchin my leg w/ my other foot n' i accidentally touched Lyles leg w/ my foot. He looked at me w/ a sort of half smile n then moved up so he was sitting up against his wall and he pulled me into his legs we were

kinda sitting like: […] It was so romantic. We were just sorta cuddling and at times he would tickle my belly or play w/ my belly ring. When the movie we were watching was over we turned off all the lights and just kinda layed there like so:

Just to let you know, I am a virgin…and I plan to keep it that way for a very long time. We cuddled and […] that's all we did tho…no kissing or nething. ☽ It's okay tho… leaves more mystery for next time. ☺ Ay yai yai… so then we just fell asleep and I left in the mornin. I didn't know if Lyle liked me or if he was just usin me but I had Lily call n say "Who do u like more, Amy or Audrey?" and he was like "I still have feelings for Audrey but after seein Amy I'm starting to like her again…cuz she was the one i originally liked but then she wanted me n Audrey to go out… ." That made me happy. I do like him, but I can't make a huge deal about it cuz Audrey would slaughter me if she found out any of this shit.

K well I'm gunna end this diary here… it was supposed to go only till the end of the summer but we've been through so much more…a lot of bad things have happened in this past week that I'm not gunna write here, partly b/c I don't want to end on a bad note and partly b/c I want to start a new diary at basically rock bottom for me. Thank u for being such an amazing diary … I've been thru so many 'firsts' w/ u… love ya ☺

    ♥ Amy

....

Amy wrote the following list on the inside cover of this journal at the end of the summer of 2004, many months after she started the journal.

SUMMA
2004
Total summer boyfriends:
- Wilhelm
- Roy
- Byron
- Gilbert

Total summer hook-ups:
- Roy
- Byron
- Kiefer G.
- Irving E.
- Gilbert
- MARIO!
- Grady

....

Amy wrote the following list on the inside cover at the end of this journal.

Lifetime Boyfriends	Lifetime hookups (make out or farther)
- Rupert J.	- Irving E. 2
- Ubange	- Rupert J. 2
- Isaiah H.	- Ubange 1
- Noah L.	- Isaiah H. 1
- Horacio H.	- Noah L. 3
- Niko	- Niko 1
- Roy	- Roy 3 sloppy
- Byron	- Byron 3
- Wilhelm	- Gilbert
- Gilbert (black)	- Monty
- Irving E.	- Kiefer G 3

- Christophe
- Edmund
- Chauncey
- (sort of) Mario

- Mario! 3
- Grady 3 sloppy
- Lyle O 3
- Kumasi (T) 3
- Paolo (T) 2
  Zeke (T) 2
- Coby – running camp 2
- **Norman Opelika 2**
- **Donovan Puebla 3**
- Edmund 3
- Chauncey 3
- Alonzo Quetta 3
- Jones

....

Amy didn't put a date on the poem that follows. It was found with her
journal entries from the end of the fall.

I'm so sorry
sorry for the pain I've caused
You've been there
Trusting me, believing.

I fucked it up
Everything you ever wanted in a child
was destroyed
The moment you found that razorblade

Words can't begin to express
How sorry I am
My heart is bleeding with guilt

For every moment you felt pain.
For every tear drop you shed,
I will make it up to you

I dedicate the rest of my life to healing your scars
And making up all the wrong I have done
It will no longer be the kiss of Judas
But the kiss of love

I love you mom

CONGRADULATIONS!

You found my diary!

Now put it down. That's right, shut it and leave it wherever you found it. Sure, you can go ahead and read it…find the 'dirt' on me…whatever..but what will you really get out of it? It won't help you like me or yourself any better. If I'm dead and you're finding this with my belongings, burn it. This is a book full of true emotion. I don't want people looking back on my life the way it's represented in this book. If I'm alive, talk to <u>me</u>. My diary is the one place in my world that I can be 100% honest with. Read one page of this and you're taking that from me. How would you feel if someone did that to you? All I'm saying is that this book contains secrets and stories that i don't feel anyone else should hear but me. You may want to know them now, but i have reason for keeping them from people. I'm asking you to please respect my privacy and leave this book alone. Thank you.

—Amy

<u>December 22, 2004[1]</u>
<u>THIS IS A DIARY ENTRY. IF ANYONE READS THIS I WILL FUCKING RUN AWAY</u>
I am writing this story out of desperation – I haven't done a diary entry in what seems like years. There's always been so much to write but I never get the chance to write it, and then it builds up.

First I'll talk about the months before now. Over the summer I had a blast. I met a boy named Mario, and really started to get my self confidence back up by spending time with boys. The popular boy from the next town over (Julian Wolds) told a bunch of the girls that used to hate me that he liked me! I had a boyfriend named Roy who totally used me.. I

---

1. Amy is almost 16.

went out with my best friend Byron, but he broke up with me because his friend [Olivia's brother] has family conflict with my family. I met a bunch of friend, like the lawn crew at my condo (Gomer, Herman, and Sargeant). I chilled with them some days on this big mulch pile, and we sometimes went out to lunch. I also met this guy Lyle Okayama at the mall.. it's a long, confusing story, but I hooked him up with my friend Audrey (even though he liked me) so I could get with his friend Jones, but then I wanted him back so we hooked up again behind Audrey's back a couple months ago. I'm such a jealos person. Like everything needs to be about me. I did the same thing to my best friend Lily J. I hooked up with Grady (this guy she liked for like 3 months) behind her back... I think it was because I wanted to prove to myself that I was as good as her. The good news is, I've realized how huge my jealousy problem is and I'm working on it. Last year for example I would tell my friends that they looked good in outfits that looked hideous just because I was jealous and I wanted to look better than them. Same with grades. It's always just been a pattern. This year I've really been working on my jealousy and also working on talking behind peoples backs. I think it's a sign of maturity, which is good.

Since the summer things have been different. There's been no more sneaking out to chill with Jones, or going to pick up a 30 rack with Lyle. Also, my relationship with my mother has changed a lot. Over the summer we were the best of friends. We got along so well and I loved it. I honestly don't know if it was because I meant it or because I knew if I sucked up I could get away with more shit. I guess it was a combination of both- I felt bad because I was lying and disobeying SO much, so I felt like I had to make it up to my parents in some way.

When the school year started Audrey and I were still like best friends in the world. We always chilled and smoked and shit. We did cross country together, and got caught smoking (our teammates told on us) half way through the season. I thought that'd be the end of my life but my parents were actually wicked chill about it. I told them it was my first time so they didn't take away anything. I mean a month later they let me spend the night alone at home while they went to my mom's marathon. Since then I've blown it though. We'll talk more about that later. Right now I'm just gonna go over some people that have played fairly major roles in my life.

Audrey: She's the girl that kinda brought out the bad in me. It's cool n everything because it's not like I didn't wanna party n shit, but she totally encouraged it. At one point, I wanted to stop my risky lifestyle, but since she was my only real friend I thought she might ditch me and I'd have no1. She calls me smokey b/c of the guy from the movie 'Friday'. At the peak of our friendship we were crazy bitches. We snuck out all the time, lied to our parents n shit. Let's talk about one of my favorite memories with her. We planned this whole breakfast thing for this one Friday before school. Our plan was to go smoke a lotta weed in the woods, then get breakfast at this little diner in her town. Her dad dropped us off, n we pretended to go sit at the diner, but then we walked down the road into the woods (it was like a 20 min walk at least!). We sat behind this rock on a trail in the woods and smoked out of a pen. The rubber was starting to melt, so we were probably smoking half rubber, but damn it was an experience. We were practicing ways to let out the smoke. She was like 'u exhale just like snoop dogg!!!'. Lol. It was priceless. Damn do I miss those days. Anyways our parents deffinetly figured out that something was going on because we got back to the diner like 2 minutes before her dad swung by and we had just gotten our coffees. We never officially got caught but my mom was SO pissed cuz Audreys mom beeped the horn right outside her classroom n she came out n saw us n it was so bad!!!!!1 She yelled at me, and Audreys mom (EMBARRASING). Audreys dad found her fuckin stash like 2 days after and flushed it down the toilet. Shit sucks.

[...] is this girl that's in my math class. She's a junior and she's a MAD druggie. She's so cool. At the beginning of the year I was like obsessed with her; I always tried to impress her and shit. She invited me to sleep over one nite but my mom was being really suspicious so she only let me go out for the night and then she called me back in at like 8 because "my dad was sick" (which she later admitted was bullshit). I went out with Sabine a couple times, like once to Chinese food which was wicked fun. I was so fucked. We swung by Audrey's ex-b/fs house and saw Big Man and talked to him for a while, then smoked out of these mad awesome pipes (I couldn't even clear my hits because they were so strong). She invited me to chill a lot (her boyfriends a coke dealer) but my mom totally knows that she's a bad influence so she won't let me n even if she did let me it wouldn't b any fun cuz my mom would drug test me the second I got home. I've also made pretty good friends with Miranda Tihuan (Sabines like best friend). She's a MAD stoner. She gets high every fucking day before school. She's wicked nice to me, like we have a study together n she's nice.

Okay so I'm totally getting off topic here. We gotta talk about what I need to get out. So, as you can see, I had a fuckin crazy life up till like a month ago. I bought 2 grams of coke for $100 then snorted it in the bathroom with Sabine and Miranda. I mean it may sound bad, but I was under control.

2 Mondays before Thanksgiving vacation I decided I wanted to do

something stupid. I brought alcohol into school. See, my brother hides his liquor supply in his desk drawers and I found it one day. Me and Audrey had been drinking it for a long time and I decided to bring dry gin in to drink during lunch (disguised in a dasani water bottle). I told Sabine about it during math and she told Miranda and Miranda came over and drank some during lunch. After lunch I was pretty buzzed. I was kinda dizzy and I was walkin around say "Yo soi Amy" (I am Amy in Spanish). Lol, I ran into this computer class at like 1:58 and started sayin it HAHA. Anyways, after school my mom came into my room and sat on my bed. She said "what would you do if someone came in and told you your daughter was drinking alcohol during lunch". I totally flipped out. I was all "that's outrageous" etc. I had this Gatorade in my backpack and I had my mom take a sip (I said it was my lunch drink). She was like "I hope I can trust you cuz I want to" and blah blah blah. The rest of the week sucked. My mom and dad got into my cell phone and started going through all my phone numbers and text messages (one of them was like "how much for one gram" or some shit). It got so bad that I had to give away alllll my shit to Miranda T. on Friday (like a gram of trees and some caff [[caffeine]] and sleeping pills). Thank God I did that b/c if I didn't I woulda been fucked. Listen to this.

Friday morning I was getting my shit outta the trunk of my moms car, and I decided to leave my purse. I thought "there's nothing bad in it so if my mom searches it she'll find nothing and trust me more". I was getting so tired and sick of the week, I just wanted it to be over. When I went upstairs to my locker, I saw a razorblade that I had used to clean out my locker. I was a cutter in 9th grade, but I stopped once my mom found out. The temptation was too much, so I took Audrey to the bathroom to talk and then went into a stall and made a few cuts on my upper arm. I swear to god I didn't do this on purpose, but when Audrey asked "What are you doing, taking a shit?" I got startled and I dropped the razorblade. Audrey was like "Amy what the hell are you doing? When Rosanne did that shit I stopped being friends with her". She ran out of the bathroom and into homeroom. She told Jemima, Mariana, Freda, and Nancy (WTF)!) and then asked me to show her my arm in front of everyone. I refused, just out of pride. We took a field trip and Nancy saw my cuts on the bus. She didn't say anything to me but she told Audrey which really pissed me off. I didn't talk to her for the rest of the day.

That afternoon on the car ride home, I noticed my mom seemed really irritated. I tried to get it out of her, but she insisted that it was nothing. When we got into the Town Center instead of going straight into the rotary we took a right, into the Town Police station. It was like the scariest moment of my life. I was like "what's this about?" to my mom and she was like "think about it, Amy". We went into the main room and waited for about 20 minutes for this police office to come out. It was so scary. I was trying to think what could be wrong. Did Miranda get caught with my stuff and rat me out? Did they find evidence of the alcohol incident? My mom kept picking up little pamphlets from this table. One for Narcotics Anonymous, one for parenting troubled teens and so on… I was so fucking nervous, it was one of the scariest moments of my life We went into this office and my mom emptied the contents of my purse (she *had* gone through it just like I suspected). Inside there was a razorblade and a little baggie. She said she thought I was doing cocaine. The officer assured her that the bag never contained coke (b/c there was no residue of any sort on the bottom of the bag). He asked me what the razorblade was for and I admitted I had used it to cut myself. He let us go after my mom talked to him in private for a while. When we got home I just went into my room and went to sleep. My mom called all my doctors and shrinks and relatives and everything. I didn't want anything to do with it. I didn't want to face what had happened during that awful week.

The next morning, I kept being woken up by the ring of our phones. My mom picked up and talked in a low, quiet voice to what seemed like dozens of people. I was still half asleep when my mom came into my room. She said "this is as late as we can let you sleep, we need to go right now though". I was like "where? Where are we going mom". She tried to avoid the subject, but then finally admitted that we were 'going to the doctors'. When I asked why she responded "because of the cutting". I quickly got dressed into my new pajama pants and a tank top, grabbed my purse and yellow sweatshirt, and went down to the car.

In the car my parents informed me that I'd been refered to City Pediatrics. I was just like omfg… We got there at like 12 and went to exam room 1 where various doctors came in and out to ask my questions and do tests on me. I got 3 blood tests, a urine test, and this weird heart test with metal stickers. Finally, at like 6 pm the doctor came in and said that my toxicality [[toxicology]] tests came out negative (thank god cuz I smoked with lyle the weekend before), but he did recommend me to be institutionalized at a psych hospital. I was scared shitless. My mom was crying her eyes out, and I was too but in private because I felt so much shame. I was taken out on a stretcher into an ambulance. It was about a 10 minute ride. I was just sitting there looking up at the ambulance roof thinking "what the fuck have I done?". We got to the hospital and the ambulance people let me walk in. (instead of being wheeled in by the stretcher). I met this lady and my parents came shortly afterwards. My parents told me they were going to search my room and my mom said "if theres anything u want to share with us, do it now". Lol-nope. I gave my parents big hugs goodbye and went into the teen unit with the lady. She sat my in a chair in the hall and I watched all the madness take place. Two really sexy black guys (about 16 or 17) were running around with boxing gloves and music blasting. People were watching movies and making phonecalls. It was MADNESS I'm telling ya. This girl, my future roommate, came up to me and she goes "Hey. I'm *crazy*. I'll tell u my crazy story later!" That actually made me feel kinda welcome. It felt like an initiation. Like I wouldn't hafta be shy. I got my heart rate and shit taken and answered like 12347195631489237 questions. Then they made me hand me all my clothes behind a door so they could search them for shit. I went around to the different rooms and got introduced to a bunch of the people. I got my purse taken away temporarily cuz I'm not allowed to wear make up till level 2 or some shit. I went into my room and talked to my roomie for like an hour. She told me how she thought she was pregnant and how she loves her boyfriend. She told me about how her moms addicted to coke and all this other stuff. I felt wicked bad. She'd only been there since the night before, but she thought she'd be getting out soon. I told her why I was there. Actually I kinda lied. I told her I was there for drugs and cutting. I was there for cutting, but not really for drugs (cuz both my tests came out negative). I was starving so they gave me turkey with gravy (which I don't eat), with diced veggies (including onions which I can't eat), and potatos. The potatos were the only thing I could bear putting into my mouth so that's what my dinner was. It was bedtime (10pm) so the nurse gave me a cup of benadryll to get me sleepy and then I went to my room. My roomie was already asleep (her meds knock her out) so I just plopped down on the bed next to her and went to sleep. What a day.

Six

Blue Locking Notebook
(later tenth grade)

1/9/05[1]

Hey … i'm really happy to be staring a new diary. So much has happened in the last few months and i always feel like i have to write it all in the same entry … anyways i've decided to just write my feelings now cuz that is what's important. My grades are really good. I haven't done drugs since November 14th. My cell phone is still confiscated b/c my parents found all these pics of me w/ boys and they're so mad. I don't have that many friends. Ever since i came back from the hospital Audrey's been wicked distant & like BFF's w/ Nancy. It feels like she totally used me over the summer. I'm getting really close w/ Lily again. I'm totally past the whole popularity thing in my grade. I only wanna be friends w/ the juniors .. they can drive and they're all mad nice. Not to be cocky but Audrey and I think some of them try to get our attention (as well as vice-versa). Like whenever we're around they seem to switch the topic onto partying and drugs. They all know that me and Audrey got suspended for smoking pot so idk… let's see… i had CCD 2day…Stuart Tablas and I had a good chat. I totally miss co-ed school. I wanna go visit my ex Horacio Hebron. I just miss the guys that weren't all about ass. I've been talking to Herman from our condo a lot… he's so adorable… he's a little chubby w/ blackish hair and a western NY accent. He seems like kind of a loser but he'd make an awesome boyfriend… idk.. I'm really into 50 cent songs now.… i'm living off the memories of the perfect life i had for about 4 months. I totally took everything for granted. Things could return back to normal some day but my parents will never trust me like they did before. Anyways i took some NyQuil so i'm pretty tired. Peace Sonny.

   ~Amy

---

1. Amy is weeks shy of 16.

January 10th, 2004 [[actually 2005]]
Not much happened today. I had a study 2nd period and it was wicked embarrassing b/c whenever i left a room three juniors were walking by it. They must've thought I was following them or something. And I was peering around this corner to see if Audrey was there and they suddenly popped up – it totally looked like i was spying on them. [...] I had a basketball game at school which i ⟦sucked⟧ at. The last one was at least fun b/c me and a junior were laughing at this huge chic from the other team. Idk what it is but I feel like i totally need to impress all the juniors. Everything I do revolves around getting them to eventually notice me. It might be b/c they have cars, or maybe b/c they're closer to my maturity level… idk. After my game Audrey and I talked to some girls from the other school and asked them if they smoked. They used to but 'not anymore'. Helena, Sally, and Trudy were giving us dirty looks…bitches. I talked to Mario online tonight. (Oh yeah my Dad unblocked by AIM!). He wants me to come to Canada w/ him next week. Yah right. He's all out for ass. Although Roy hurt me in so many ways I did gain a very good thing out of our relationship - - knowledge. I'm much more awake now when i talk w/ guys. I can analyze what they're out for. Mario's a mad sexy (even April Aube said) 18 yr old from Conneticit and i went to 2nd base w/ him the first day i met him. He wants sex. He's not getting it. I'm much better off w/ a Herman type. I'm so lonely. I want love so bad, but i'm not gonna let myself be tricked again into thinking a boy likes me when he's just out for ass. Oh well. I need to figure out my life priorities. I scored in the 92% on the PSATs! Yay me. Oh, i'm trying to get all A's so i can make principal's list. Wish me luck! That would blow people's minds ☺ Night, Pepe [[people]]

~Amy

January 11th 2005
My life is so boring. I do the same thing every day. School – Practice – Homework – Bed. B/c i am surrounded by only girls i become infatuated with being popular. I seriously thought I was bi for a while b/c I'm totally obsessed w/ impressing the popular juniors. I talked to a few boys today though, and it's just a totally different feeling. It's so much more of a deep, unexplainable emotion when i talked to my friend Julian Wolds for example. He's from the next town over and we liked each other at the end of the summer. I feel wicked comfortable talking to him. Like sometimes i feel like he's bullshitting me just b/c he uses such deep words. His g/f dumped him so that was sad. He like really liked her. He told me I'm a nice girl and then

signed off. I need to go to a co-ed school. All girls is fucking with my head so bad. I talked to Audrey on the phone for like an hour. She is still obsessed w/ her freshman boyfriend, Abe. Good for her I wish I could be that happy. ☹ I've matured so much though since the summer. I was such an insecure slut. If I saw the old me today I would feel bad for me. Idk and just like w/ everything in school (i barely gossip anymore) at home (i apologize when i mess up instead of keeping my 'pride'). I had a 45 minute conversation with Sister Juliann today. We talked about my connection w/ Jesus. She said I should try praying more and familiarizing myself w/ Jesus so i'm not just talking when i want something. She's so wise, but she's getting old. Well I'm mad tired so i'm out. Peace. ~ Amy

January 12th, 2004 [[really 2005]]

Ah it's so late. I've been getting so little sleep lately it's uncanny. I'm thinking about taking my mom to the mother / daughter event at school. Even though she sometimes drives me crazy, i definitely over-react when i'm mad at her. I've put her through so much pain in the past few years. She worked her ass off throughout her school-time so she could have a happy life and i'm ruining that for her. I think it'd mean a lot to her if i like surprised her or something w/ school concert tickets for her birthday.

Today was overall okay. Audrey wasn't in school. Most people were late to school b/c they thought it'd be a snow day.

I literally count down the days until 'away' basketball games b/c they are an opportunity to get to know the juniors (from the bus ride). There was one 35 miles away today. (*FUNNY – Tennise D. going under bleachers to get Tracey's book, then her brace!). I called up Lyle Okayama who I haven't talked to for 2 months. We talked awkwardly for a minute and then he said he had to go "hey can i give u a call back later?'. He's not gonna be calling back. Anyways Tennise D. wanted to see his picture so I showed her my photos and before I knew it the whole varsity team was crowding around my pictures like "how old is he?" "is he your boyfriend?". The fat chick was like 'c'mon Amy - - spill". I felt mad cool for a little while ☺ Esp. b/c before that I thought everyone hated me and i opted not to play in the game b/c I was scared people would make fun of me. idk i was thinking a lot about Julian W. today. I kinda still do have feelings for him (even though we've only met twice). We talked a little more online tonight. It wasn't as smooth as last night's convo but w/e. Damn I'm like unbelievably tired... i'll ttyl. ☺

~ Amy

January 13th, ~~2004~~ [2005]

Sup? Dude idk what's wrong w/ me. I'm seriously willing to do anything to become popular w/ the juniors. I was gonna drink half a bottle of Robitussen 2mrw so i could be high in front of them in a study i have w/ them. I tell myself that popularity isn't worth shit but i don't act it. I'll work on it. My b-day's in one week from today ☺ I have therapy at 5pm and i get to bring Audrey. Speaking of Audrey, i'm going to the diner 2mrw after school with her and Sherryl and Maynard Y and Abe (Audreys boyfriend). That should be fun. This junior that buys coke - - i think to impress ppl but shes MAD cool - - IMed me today. And oh, I thought Sabine like hated me b/c she hasn't been as nice lately but today she invited me to go see this guy with her and Miranda T. I had bball [[basketball]] practice though (unfortunately). See, i've always been fine w/ social situations and shit. Like when people get to know me they tend to keep asking me to chill or whatever but my problem is i'm too afraid to even talk to people. I hate being dependant on Audrey for my 1 friend b/c she only cares about boys and drugs, not her friends. OK imma sleep.

    - Amy

January 14th, 2005

Omg… there seems to be a pattern in my life… every day <u>just before</u> a holiday / vacation i get in some kind of trouble. Friday before Thanksgiving I was taken to the police station and then Saturday I was taken to the hospital. The Friday just before Christmas vacation i was taken out of school to get drug tested b/c my guidance counselor is a psycho. Today is the Friday before Martin Luther King day weekend. OK so today Audrey and I planned to go to "the diner" right after school. We'd have Audrey's friends (Abe & Maynard) pick us up and drive us there. Then we'd all head back and chill at school before the basketball game (@ 6). Well since i'm not allowed to hang out w/ Audrey i told my mom i was going w/ Sherryl (and we brought her along just in case we were checked on). Anyways everything was going smooth until we got to the diner. Abe started making this huge deal about how he didn't want so many people in the car. Then Audrey was like "guys, we'll come back." She's like 'get the hell out'. we were both just kinda like 'ok' but we got out. They didn't come back for an hour and when they finally did i totally bitched out Audrey. I was all like 'this is why you have no friends - - cuz u only care about guys and ur self". She was a total bitch to Sherryl. See, Sherryl and I had a talk over our meal about what Audrey does and how she uses people. Sherryl goes 'We're so mad at u Audrey' and then Audrey is like "i don't give a shit about you Sherryl". What a hag. Then we all got a ride back to the school from Maynard. We drove around 2ce b/c Coach was there the first time we went around. Then we got out at the side entrance and Audrey was like 'guys i'm gonna go chill w/ Maynard & Abe.' I was like excuse me? I told her that this was it. If she left now i'd never be her friend again. She gave me the middle finger, then waved in a very provoking way. That just set me off. I hate her so much. I've never been able to ditch her before but now it's different. She can rot in hell for all i care. Then she came back @ like 5:30 and waved to me but i didn't respond. Her, Maynard, and Abe all hung out and played bball on one side of the court. I had a really bad game so when it was over i just walked out. The thing that pissed me off though was that this really popular freshman girl knows Abe and she was talking to him. What if she starts chilling w/ Audrey and gets all her cool Juniors to like her too? Whatever. OK so anyways I got home and I was on my computer and then my mom came in and she's like "i need to see u downstairs right now". i went down and she gave me a pen & paper and made me write a list of all the things i did after school. Apparently someone had told her that i was doing some kind of shit before my basketball game. When I came upstairs my mom was searching my room!!! I was like OMFG! Then she made me give her all the clothes I wore after school so she could see how wet they are and smell them for smoke. The thing is I really wasn't smoking or drinking. I told my mom I'd called her from the diner but she claimed she'd never recieved a call or message (which is bullshit). I'm <u>so</u> pissed b/c the 1 time me and Audrey could've hung out in like a month she ditched me for a freshman that looks like he's 10 and an Asian looking Puerto Rican. I'm not taking her back. I don't give a fuck how much I'll miss her.. i'm sick of her SHIT. And now my mom thinks i'm guilty of something i didn't do? Im pissed.

    ~Amy.

January 15th, 2005

OMG. so this morning I woke up to my mom standing over my bed. She goes 'I owe you a HUGE apology'. Turns out she'd rechecked her messages and found the one from me! Then my dad came and invited me to breakfast (which I of course accepted). Before we left I wanted to call Audrey just to say "hey i don't like you but i'm just calling to warn you that we might be in trouble". I never got the chance to do that. My therapist called and we talked for a couple minutes. He told me my mom had called but he <u>didn't know why</u> and he wanted to talk to her for a couple minutes. I decided to listen in on the other phone. As soon as they started talking Dr. DeSantos was like "So what are you worried she was doing last night?" He lied to me about not knowing why my mother called. On top of that he suggested that my mom keep a 'standing' blood test w/ the doctors so she could take me on-demand. That just fuckin pissed me off. I trusted Dr. DeSantos _so_ much. I was even a little attracted to him. I can't believe it. Who can I trust in this world of liars? Anyways I had oboe later which was fine. It reminded me of summer when I was carefree. OK well I'm gunna go... I just wanted to fill you in (no pun intended) on the situation. Peace.

    -Amy

1/16/05

Hey. I'm pissed off at Julian. I seriously thought he was such a nice guy and such good boyfriend material. Like no joke we've had some awesome conversations. I totally feel like he gets me. Anyways tonight we were talking about using people. He's all like "its fine to use girls... it feels good on my dick". I was like "do u know what that does to a girls emotions?". Guys just don't get that by pleasuring themselves for 30 seconds they could be ruining someones life. Oh and I also thought that Julian was a virgin. Tonight he told me he's slept w/ like 5 girls... I'm not attracted to that at all. I just find it astonishing. You think someone is one way the whole time you know them and then one day they just totally overturn it. He acts so different when he's around guys like Grady. Maybe someone was at his dorm. Will I ever find the right guy for me?

    ♥ Amy

January 18th 2005

Hey... My sister left for college yesterday. I kinda miss her.. Today I had a basketball game. Sally & I were gunna go to the diner (b/c the game wasn't till 6) but it was _so_ cold outside so we ordered pizza instead. The fat chic was all like "I woulda given you guys a ride if i had my car!". This senior, Helena's sister, came to sit and eat w/ me and Sally. She's really nice. We all talked for like ½ an hour and then this black like 25 yr old guy walks in. He's the dude that fills the vending machines. We're tight. I always used to see him at lunch and during studies. I told him back in October how I got suspended and he was like "did you stop?" and i was like NO! and he was like "girrrl we got to chillllll". Anyways this time he walked in and I was like "hey" and he was like "sup? you still smoking weed?". I was like "hell yah!". It was right in front of Sally, Helena's sister, and this other athlete. He told me now he tries not to smoke but he can't help himself. Then I scuffled over and told him how I "went to detox' and he was like "aw that sucks". He gave us some free candy then left. Sally and Helena's sister were all like 'how did u know that guy?' I'm kinda happy cuz now that Helena's sister knows she might tell more ppl from my team. I need to maintain my stoner rep. Then we had a bball game which i didn't play in at all bcuz i skipped Martin Luther King day. The coach <u>made</u> me go into the girls locker room to fix my shirt. When I went in it was the fat chick, the blonde chick, this other girl, and Helena's sister. I swear i turned like dark purple I was <u>so</u> embarrassed and self conscious. [...] They prolly [[probably]] talked about me after (idk if it was in a good or bad way but w/e). Well i gtg…peace   ~Amy

January 19th, 2005

Had a field trip today. Went to see the glass menagerie. It amazes me how immature ppl can be. Like, they were laughing at one of the guys cuz they thought he was gay. It just shows how much more mature I've gotten to be. Audrey and I still haven't talked at all cept' for being forced lab partners on Monday. I've come to realize I <u>can</u> live w/out her. Her and Nancy plan to go to the diner on Friday. I was ½ considering telling on them (b/c they plan to smoke) but what would that do for anyone? After school I had Sherryls brother pick me up n drive me around the school again blasting his music. He has a g/f but w/e i'm fine w/ it…dude the fat chic got injured! I feel bad.. she was like Varsitys best player. Tonight I went snowboarding in my yard. It was fun… I'm getting a lot better ☺ My mom watched me the whole time. Yah so nothing else really happened. My B-DAY 2mrw! 😄Peace.

-A.C.

CRAZY THINGS I DID WHEN I WAS 15

- Went to spring training w/ my dad
- Smoked pot for the first time (w/ Lyle)
- Met Gomer, Sargeant, Herman (lawn boys in at our condo)
- Smoked with Valentine's Dad
- Small party in Jones' attick
- Stole a pipe from Jones' house
- Slept over Lyles house
- met Mario (w/ Art + Ship)
- Got suspended for smoking pot before XC [[Cross Country]]
- Became best friends w/ Audrey
- Drank w/ Grady, Julian, Lily
- Hook ups: Grady, Mario, Roy, Irving, Lyle
- Almost got pregnant (Roy) + mom found out
- went to teen psych ward for cutting
- Accused of coke problem by parents
- drug tested by school
- crazy nights w/ Sabine; car swerve; Chinese food
- Got my belly button pierced
- When parents away – party with Peyton, Reynold, Audrey near the mall
- Got record for detentions in school

January 20th 2004 [[really 2005]]
My birthday! Yay! It's so nice to have people recognize you and say 'con-gradulations'. not for doing anything; merely because you're alive. Nancy got me a pink necklace w/ a heart and a huge crown ring. My mom and I went to get my permit and we waited for over half an hour on these hard wooden benches just to find out we didn't have the proper ID. We had a passport but apparently a birth certificate was needed. I was so pissed. I had an appt w/ Dr. DeSantos today at 5. I totally gave him the cold shoulder for what he said to my mom but by the end I opened back up. Mom, Dad and I just had cake and ice cream. I got earrings, a car repair book that I wanted, salon shampoos, a snowboard (☺) and some stuff from my other relatives. Overall a great b-day. IM 16! ~Amy

1/21/04 [[really 05]]
Hey! sup? Just got back from a bball game @ Broton. Our starting Center got injured so Coach played me the whole 2nd half and I scored. Yay. I asked one of the Broton coaches if he knew a couple ppl (Calvin Dodona etc) and he was like 'yah. Know Dodona?' Then Trudy goes 'omg Amy you seriously know EVERYONE'. Dayum straight ☺ Let's see not too much happened earlier today. Omg tho - - in science we had to do groups of 4 and I refused to be w/ Audrey so me and Jemima and Sherryl worked w/ and this other girl; she and I have become a lot closer over the past few weeks. Today she totally sketched me out tho. I was standing at my lab bench observing pla-nateria when she came up and tickled me on my sides, awfully close to my breasts. She is openly bi-sexual so I was seriously really disturbed and taken aback. I felt violated and like I was gunna throw up for a long ass time. Oh I also got my permit. I look wicked bad in my picture but its all good. I drove home which was a blast. Ohh [[oh]]. 1 more thing - - the blonde chick talked to me a little today. She commented on my purse and then she went thru it a little and we talked. she goes "why is this sequin off?". i explained how my mom had ripped it off while searching my purse. She goes 'Oh.. watd [[what did]] she find – marijuana?" I was like "maybe… u smoke? She nodded her head. Hey at least we can understand each other on that level. Nite. ~Amy

1/23/045
Hey. Not much has been goin on. Went out to breakfast again w/ my dad yesterday. There was a huge storm from 5 pm yesterday till 6pm today. Newscasters were all over it. "The Blizzard of 05'" they called it. Well the

good news is school got cancelled for 2mrw. It was so cool b/c i was the first kid to find out (cuz my moms a teacher) so i put it up on my away msg. Carolina Bucara IMed me and was like 'ahh are you serious?!". She's friends w/ all the juniors and when i told her i wasn't JK [[Just Kidding]] suddenly they had it on their away msgs. It wasn't even on the news yet b/c the principal had just called it off. Coincidence? I think not. Cool ☺ Peace! ~Amy

January 24th, 2005

Hey. As I said, no school today. I was supposed to go snowboarding with Lily but she invited this other girl (who I absolutely love but I know I'm not as good as them at snowboarding) so I cancelled. I stayed home with my mom instead. One thing I love about my mother is that no matter how angry or upset she is, she'll always make time to hug me. She let me drive her around the block 2 times which wasn't bad. O.M.G. [[Oh My God]] guess who called at like 4 though? Lyle! He's the guy that I sort of hooked up with .. my main acquaintance near our condo. After I slept over his house in November I went to the hospital and I hadn't talked to him since. Audrey had said she'd talked to him a little and he was 'gunna come visit her'. I call him from friends cell phones but usually he's not home or he can't talk. I was just fucking amazed that he not only thought of me, but went through all the trouble of finding my <u>house</u> phone #. (I'd only given him my cell in the past). We talked for like 20-30 minutes. Apparently he's dropped out of school. This kid told that Lyle was selling drugs and put a court-enforced restraining order on him so Lyle will go to jail for even looking at the kid. Omg I'm so sad, he might be moving to Texas. ☹. He wants to move b/c he already found a job there installing windows for $15/hour. That'd SUCK majorly if he left but i guess i'll never understand the situation he's in and the decisions he has to make. He asked me when I was coming back up to the condo and I said maybe 1-2 weekends. I miss seeing him. I miss the summer. God, I can never stress it enough: YOU DON'T KNOW WHAT YOU GOT TILL ITS GONE. Well, i'm goina sleep. Nite.

    ~Amy.

1/31/05

Nobody gets me. And I'm <u>not</u> just saying that to be pessimistic. Today I was listening to the song 'Over' by Lindsay Lohan. It was talking about how this girl can't get this one guy out of her head and how she thinks about him day and night. At first I was thinking 'hm…. i can totally relate to this song'. I've always had one guy or one person i've been literally obsessed with. I was trying to think of one person, anyone, that i couldn't stop thinking about. And I drew a blank. Seriously there isn't one person in my life right now that i feel like i can always turn to on anything. The first name that popped into my head was Mario. That thought was soon discarded when I realized I don't like Mario any more then a friend. Sure, he's someone i talk to and flirt with a little online but I mean we've never had an in depth conversation. We're always talking about making plans to see each other (which never follow through) or what pictures to send each other. I'm sick of having superficial talks with amateurs that only care about 'hooking up' or 'how their weekend was'. I want someone - - anyone - - who i can have a really deep conversation with about real issues. I'm so sick of changing for guys. My whole life I've changed the way i dress, my friends, my behavior, my morals… even the pitch of my voice all for the sake of attracting and impressing members of the opposite sex. For once I want a connection with someone that doesn't take me being fake to develop. Guys like Mario -> why'd i go for them? B/c they are the stereotypical 'hot' and i blinded myself from the fact that they might not be my type at all for two key reasons. #1 (and this is the biggest by far) to impress people. I always figured if i brought in pictures of me and my hot guys, and if i was always talking to my men on the phone, people would be impressed. I gave up my own marital status just for a failed chance at becoming popular. I turned myself into pretty much a slut in an attempt to lessen my insecurities. It worked. For a little while. But when the summer fun's over and you've kissed your last boy goodbye—what do you have left? If you're with a boy like i was with you're left with a bad rep, torn emotions, and a couple 'good' memories. If you are lucky enough to have a boy that really and truly cares about you… you are the luckiest person in the world. You're left w/ everything a person could ever wish for. Happiness. Love. That's what I want but i don't know if it's ever gonna happen. I don't know if theres one boy out there that could really understand me <u>and</u> care about me, but i'll keep optimistic and pray that if my Mr. Right is out there somewhere, i will eventually find him.

    - Amy

February 4th, 05

Blah. Kinda shitty day. Had a basketball game. The fat chick showed up w/ her boyfriend (who is actually pretty damn sexy). I did get my cell back tho (for the weekend). I was making a fool out of myself calling like 845,976 people b/c my cell phone's a total security blanket. I forgot to take my meds last night so the whole day I was totally feeling like all dizzy and depressed.

Oh, earlier this week I talked to this kid (friends w/ Juliette Efate). He seems cool, he's supposed to sell me orange weed and acid but idk if he's all talk. Anyways we were supposed to meet up @ Lilys for the superbowl but now Lily wants to go to this guys house so its all fuckd. Peace. –AMY

Feb. 16th, 04 [[really 05]]
Hey. I know I haven't written in a while. I've been busy w/ school n stuff. Audrey and I made up. She wrote a message on my locker that was like 'i may be mad @ u but u r [[you are]] still a [...] 2 me'. So now we're cool. Idk what else is up. I've been thinking about life a lot lately. Way too much to write, but idk.. i'm just glad I'm alive. I had oboe 2day. My teacher told me i wouldn't be ready for the audition for an orchestra. Oh well. My English teacher made a point that i've been pondering. She's like "you don't remember material things only the experiences you've had'. This is so true. I need to get out more. My life is passing by and i'm letting it go by. Well i gtg
♥ Amy

~FEBRUARY VACA~
I got to Florida Saturday night. Me n' Mom got a little lost on the way to our relatives but we found it. Sunday I just kinda lazed around in the sun (attempting to get a really dark tan like last year). I've realized that I look kinda good w/ my hair in a real high ponytail so i wore it like that when me n my mom walked down to big slice pizza for lunch (where the chef was kinda lookin at me). Monday we all drove down to the Mets Spring Training. Tuesday Mom left to go to Texas. I did a little tanning + swimming. Its cool that I have boobs now cuz I can go to the pool w/out feelin all self-conscious. Tuesday night I decided to walk down to the plaza. I wore a mini skirt with a tank top. When I was walking down the driveway this car pulled up next to me n this like 18 year old guy (who was actually pretty good looking) was like 'sup girl?' I was like 'nothing'. Then he goes 'Hey by any chance are you 18?" I was like "Oh, I'm 16". Then he said something to whoever he was talking to on his cell phone n' slowly drove off. At the bottom of the driveway there were these boys on skateboards, about my age, who kinda checked me out n' were like 'whos that'! I didn't answer. I was shy, ok! Then I walked into the plaza n there were all these guys on rollerblades, bikes, n skateboards. One of them (who looked almost exactly like Lyle Okayama) walked his dog like rite next to me but I kinda just blew him off. Then, later, I walked past them at Burger King and a cute boy w/ curly blonde hair waved to me n i waved back but i just kept walking. [...]

The next few days I just kinda hung out and read some books. Thursday I went to a carnival w/ my relative. I wore shorts and a tank top (so it wasn't <u>too</u> slutty). A lot of boys were checking me out. I went on this spaceship ride where the ride operators were smoking cigarettes in the middle. Before I walked out I asked this guy (who looked kind of like Ryan Phillipe in Cruel Intentions) if he smoked trees n he said yah. I asked if he had any but he said no. Then he asked how old I was n when I told him i was 16 he was like "oh damn". I saw the same guy as we were leaving. We made eye contact like 50 times from when I was on my last ride until he was out of sight. He was just standing on the ride he was helping with and looking at me. Whenever I looked back he was still looking. It was <u>SO</u> sweet. Oh ya i think it was Wednesday night when i was feeling kinda horny. I talked to Mario online (from my cell phone) n we were talkin all dirty… I'm pretty sure it was cybersex but im not positive. Oh me n Julian Wolds have been talking a lil bit. Idk bout him tho … we'll see. Well that's about it:… PEACE!

~AMY

PRE-TASTE OF CHAOS + TASTE OF CHAOS

Got back from FL. Not that tanned ꙷ. Lily came over Saturday night n we went to the mall. I got my cartlidge pierced! Its cute. Got lots of clothes for the concert - - we might be driving these Boys Norman and his buddy, and some others (from RPHS). Wicked nervous and excited. Nite of the concert came (didn't drive the boys ☹) It was a lot of fun. I did NO drugs but I honestly didn't care that much. I went in the mosh pit a lot n' I lost my shoe in there! It was fucked up. I got hit on a lil but by mostly pretty ugly guys. I'd be walking up the stair n here 'ur gorgeous' or 'ooo la la'. I met up w/ Audrey, Rosanne Ubangi, this guy, and Nancy there. Audrey gave me a vicaden [[Vicodin]] which turned out to not be a vicadin. Saw this guy who's kinda cute. Nite.

–AC

Mario.

Hey. Mario came up today to see me! He brought Bud and Art which was cool. I had my mom drop me off @ the plaza b/c "i was looking for a semi dress". I was kinda mean to Mario, like I wouldn't face him n I hugged him last outta everyone. I admit I was being rude, but that's only b/c when I saw Mario I was like "OMFG I AM NOT HOT ENOUGH FOR HIM". Lets see…. oh I had Bud buy me some vodka. Then we drove to the other side of the city. We got kinda lost n' ended up just going to Applebees. OMG it was so nerve racking b/c we were in the city trying to find our way back to the plaza and my mom keeps calling to try to figure out when she can pick me up. I was absolutely freaking out. We finally got back to the plaza bur Mario still wasn't speaking to me. I'd called Kenneth to see if he could get me some coke, and Mario was apparently pissed. I met w/ Kenneth, gave him $60 ($10 for weed $50 for coke) n then I tried to talk to Mario but he didn't wanna hear it. I gave him a hug goodbye n' re-united w/ my mom. Later Mario told me he was pissed for the coke thing, but also b/c i was 'always on my phone w/ someone' or talking about another guy. I apol, gized to him n' we agreed that the next time we see each other it'll be much better. We also talked about our habits and he agreed to try to quit smoking if i stopped coke ☺. See ya.

-Amy

SOPHOMORE SEMI!

Was soooooooo much fun. I went w/ Ricardo Kumasi, Ricardo Zutphen, and Monty Waadt. (Ricardo K. and Monty ended up going w/ Nancy n' Audrey). Both Ricardos are like really popular at RPHS. Ricardo Kumasi is pretty attractive, Ricardo Zutphen is like so baby cute!

Catholic schools often have annual class retreats for bonding and reflection. During Amy's sophomore retreat, one assignment was to fill a box with objects representing different aspects of personal health and wellness. Amy wrote the index cards that follow to describe the objects she put in her box.

Sophomore Retreat Cards (Spring 2005)

I received my BVMP varsity letter for my participation in the 2004-2005 cross country season. I had not been on any real teams before I joined at BVMP but I grew to love it and I know I will keep dedicated to it throughout my high school career. Not only is it good for my physical health, I actually enjoy doing it.

Broton Crossings (represented by the business card) is a senior living community in which I work on weekends. I started out volunteering in 8th grade for a community service project, but once I got to know the residents and staff I decided I couldn't leave. Working at Broton Crossings affects my social health. I used to think of the elderly as almost 'boring', but now I've realized just how fun they can be. During the past 2 years I've formed relationships with more people there than I ever knew possible. The residents at Broton Crossing are always teaching me new things both about school and life. They give me insight on different issues I actually *want* to learn about (which contributes to my intellectual wellness).

If you look around the border of the bottom part of my box you can see a few different math symbols and characters. Since math is my favorite subject, I decided it was appropriate to include it in my box. I'm not exactly the best student in my math class, but I really do enjoy solving problems. Math contributes to my intellectual health because my dedication to it makes me a more learned person.

Inside my box I've included the lyrics to one of my favorite songs (Hold On by Good Charlotte). The lyrics represent my love of music. Music greatly affects my emotional health. Whenever I'm upset, angry, or stressed out I can subdue my emotions simply by popping my favorite CD in my Discman. I chose "Hold On' to put into my box because it was made me emotionally stronger on multiple occasions. Listening to it makes me realize that everyone has problems, and one should not let these problems overtake his life. Music has the power to calm me down, cheer me up, and bring out an array of different feelings. It is a very significant contributor to my emotional health.

The blue cross inside my box is a gift I received for my Confirmation from my sponsor, Sister Juliann. It has a medal of Saint Augustine (who I chose as my patron saint) intertwined with the beads. Being confirmed was very important to me because it officially declared me as part of the adult catholic community. It helps my spiritual health because now I'm responsible for helping to set an example for the youth in the Catholic community. The more years that pass, the more I hope to grow closer to God.

My 'Padi' open water diving license is something I earned when I completed a scuba diving program. Not a lot of people know that I scuba dive, but I consider it one of my hobbies. Scuba diving is good for my physical and social health because I am exercising while meeting new people from around the country (during my scuba diving vacations).

When I grow up I'm hoping to be a pediatrician (which is what the picture of the doctor with the baby represents). I'm going to a medical program this summer to shadow all sorts of doctors and see what the profession is like. This will be very good for my intellectual health because I will be learning new things and participating in an educational program that most kids my age won't get to experience.

The reed inside my box is there to represent my oboe playing. I've been playing the oboe since about 4th grade. The oboe is a very important part of my life, even though most people don't even know that I play. Playing the oboe affects my spiritual health. I play in the church youth band, and I find music is the best way for me to get in touch with God. It's almost like my own personalized way of praying. Being in the band also affects my social wellness because I'm always meeting new friends and starting amazing friendships through my involvement in it.

The 1st place ribbon is a replica of a ribbon I received in 6th grade for skateboarding at [...] (I didn't want to put the real one in because it's framed in my room and I wouldn't want anything to happen to it). Skateboarding *is* good for my physical health, but it is also important for my emotional health. Skateboarding is often looked upon as a 'boys' sport and it took a lot of confidence for me to stand up and be one of the only girls in town to do it. Bring successful has boosted my self-esteem, making skateboarding a critical contributor to my emotional health.

The 'footprints' prayer is included in my box because it is one of my favorites. I pray a lot which helps my spiritual health by strengthening my relationship with God. I received this copy of the prayer when I went on retreat with my church. It reminds me how much God loves us

There is a gap of almost one year in Amy's journals from the end of sophomore year until the spring of junior year. However, her list of "CRAZY THINGS I DID WHEN I WAS 16" captures her continued experimentation through much of that time. During the summer she was away for over five weeks: visiting our friends in Hawaii, participating in the National Youth Leadership Forum on Medicine (NYLF), and training at cross country camp (with Audrey).

Amy chose to return to BVMP, was elected co-captain of the cross country team, worked a part-time receptionist job at the auto school, and made the first-quarter honor roll. In March 2006, I found a Vicodin in Amy's purse, a marijuana baggie under her bed, and alcohol. She had also begun taking Adderall, having convinced her second psychiatrist that she had Attention Deficit Disorder (ADD). Adderall, like Ritalin, is a prescription stimulant used in treating ADD.

In April, Amy decided to join a mission trip to the Gulf Coast to help rebuild after Hurricane Katrina. On that trip she met her new boyfriend, Alonzo, who also went by Lon.

CRAZY THINGS I DID WHEN I WAS 16

- […]
- got my license
- got pulled over w/ Audrey's ex, Christophe, Liza + some chic (after Chad deal)
- got caught sneaking out @ Lilys (to see Mario)
- Did lots of drugs: Matthew, Mikey, Steve [[marijuana]] (obv.), Chad, Nancy [[cocaine]]
- tried to go snowboarding w/ Liza
- Hook-ups: Mario, Edmund, Christophe, Paolo (NYLF), Norman, Kumasi, Zeke, Coby, Liam
- Got my tongue pierced. Then took it out.
- Drove drunk (2ce)
- Dealt w/Miranda when she slept over (Alcohol poisoning)
- Made a sconex [[high school social networking site that shut down in 2008 because it could not compete with Myspace and Facebook]] and a myspace
- Sophomore semi w/ Kumasi, RZutphen, + Monty
- Had drinks w/ my dad's friend's wife in Hawaii
- Fun hook-up w/ Zeke (151; coming back to hotel @ 2AM)
- Meeting college guys at bar in Hawaii
- Buying + tripping on shrooms at NYLF ceremony and we won award
- Partying w/ my brother + my sister in the midwest
- Saw the movie "Hostel'
- Hung out w/ my sister's friend; […]
- Cross Country camp with Audrey
- Indiana with my NYLF friend (his friend's mom almost smoked w/ us) + munchies
- Michigan with my NYLF girlfriend; hot tub blazing, beer pong
- Got kicked out of Helena Mead's party
- Had text message sex with Mario
- Had phone sex with Norman
- Became captain of XC team
- Got job at Broton Auto School
- Started taking Aderall
- Stayed @ Waldorf Astoria w/ Nancy in NY; bought pipe
- Saw: Chad Michael Murray, Gary Payton, Star Jones
- ~~Downloaded gay porn~~

Seven
Red Marble Composition Notebook
(end of junior year)

Hey there, May 17th, 06[1]

Right now I'm sitting on my bed watching 'My Super Sweet 16' on MTV. I've been thinking about Lon a lot. Lon's this boy I met when I went to volunteer on the Gulf Coast over April Break. Hilary Abaco was really into him at first [...] then Lon and I started getting close and he made it clear that he wanted to at least hook up with me. This was all back in April when I was still dating Chauncey, so I didn't cheat, but Lon and I sat together on the plane rides back and that was a lot of fun... I guess you could say we 'bonded' haha. When we got back to MA [[Massachusetts]] I didn't really expect anything to happen since Lon goes to RPHS, and like everyone there hates me. But since then we've been talking pretty much consistently every day, usually for like 2- 5 hours on the phone or internet. It's nice to have a guy who actually has time for me when we're not physically together ... it's sweet. Anyways, when I saw Chauncey back in MA (he came to my Jr. prom) I just didn't feel the connection w/ him. I don't know if it's because I had feelings for Lon or b/c he wasn't being very flirtatious himself, but we ended up breaking up the next week. Lon and I actually hooked up in my parents bed a while ago ... I was home sick, so I picked him up from school and we chilled at my house. I don't know how I felt about the hook-up... I mean, on 1 level, he's an awesome guy and I'm really attracted to him, but then I also see him as just a friend ... like a buddy to hang out and go shopping with. I guess we kind of have a "thing" (as Lon would say)

---

1. Amy is 17.

5/31 06

- Lily's house after school w/ Lon + this other guy
- Intoxicated wrestling – Lon and I like it rough ☺; cuddled on couch, watched Mr. Deeds
- Lily started tweaking out; felt wicked drunk;
★ Lon starts hugging Lily, grabbing her ass (intensely) while the other guy and I clean up basement mess
- Lily and I go upstairs b/c we're supposed to leave when her mom does
- Starts puking; half passes out on bed
- I go yell @ boys for hitting on lily when she was so shitty [[drunk or high]]; both deny; I make them hide bottle + cups + vacuum room
- Lily's mom comes home; very suspicious
- Story about Lily being upset about poo
- Boys leave
- Mrs. Jackson and I end up talking for over an hour about boys etc.
← BONDING!
- I go home ~8; very pissed @ Lon; i like him but can't trust him; will confront him 2mrw.

– Amy

Essay about Gulf Coast Experience

After three and a half years at a high school with a total enrollment of less than two hundred, I've become very familiar with (and expectant of) strong and effective leadership. This may have been the reason for my response to the virtual absence of leadership during a volunteer program I participated in last April. I arrived...with a group of 20 adults and teenagers who hoped to help rebuild the Gulf Coast after Hurricane Katrina. While none of us knew exactly what to expect, we could not have predicted that the volunteer center at which we lodged would be almost as disorganized and devastated as the town. With two adult leaders in charge of a camp of about 150 people, simply retrieving job assignments was chaotic enough; actually making it to work sites and carrying out tasks in an orderly manner was nearly impossible. While many were discouraged, given the circumstance, others used this as an opportunity to take the initiative and become leaders. I worked with other members from my group to organize various methods of transportation to work sites and sanitize molding garments. At the school where we were cataloging donated library books, the librarian was clearly new to her job, but based on our experience of having grown up around well organized libraries we were able to make effective suggestions to help the process move forward. Eventually a group of about forty people had merged to create an effective working environment. The experience was so unique because there were no power struggles between adults and teenagers; everyone was a leader and everyone was doing the best he or she could to rebuild the town. From this experience I not only tested my ability as a leader but also gained the confidence in my leadership that I'll need for college and beyond.

Midwest Biology Research Summer Program

On June 17th 2006, Amy left for a four-week biology research program in the Midwest. Because she hoped to pursue a medical career, this course seemed like a good choice academically. Amy's father and I also hoped she would benefit from being with a new group of friends during the summer, which had always been a vulnerable time for her. However, the day before she left, her psychiatrist called to report a positive toxicology screen for cocaine, which set the stage for her journal entries as well as other documents included below.

6/17

- Arrived @ the Midwest Biology Research Summer Program (BRSP)
- met some cool peeps (suitemates 1 + 2)
- this guy Tully who's in 2nd yr BRSP, smokes lines
- neighbors 1 + 2
- In past week:
  - rollercoaster w/ Lon; it's over now; took me out of his prof ('foxy laday')
  - drug tested Monday
  - positive for coke – deny or admit?
- still really miss Lon whenever I see his pics; things just too competitive @ end;
  - this 9th grader 'hitting on him'; date for frosh formal; me going away just ruined it all
- had intense hook ups; before (when we were just friends) he sort of put me on a pedistool [[pedestal]]. Now that he's seen me naked n done lots of shit w/ me, i'm not a challenge anymore. I'm just another girl who wants Lon Quetta.
- no calls; 1 missed last night; none since
- first guy since middle school i think i genuinely liked; (and who genuinely liked me). ☹
- I have to really take advantage of my time here in the midwest
- who knows what life will be like when I get back?
  - Amy

6/19 – 6/25
★ Tully = friend only
  - studied together in upstairs lounge
  - listened to Gnarles Barkley + Bad Touch
  - idk what turned me off of him (smelly?).
  - now he's having sex w/ this chill girl from "Louisiana"
★ Talked to Calvin D. 3 times
  - interesting convo 1st time
    - Calvin's Mom answer "omg is this the gorgeous tall girl? You should think about modeling…I like her.." really 'smooth' convo
  - last night talked again w/ Edmund too
  - Indian restaurant when I get back

★ Boys @ this university
 - not very many attractive girls
 - ~10 fairly cool boys ➜
 1. Pliny – Tully's fuckbuddy's friend; very nice, adorable; walked around 6 flags w/ him today; too innocent?
 2. Very chill kid from the West Coast; taking Human Rights + Japanese History; pretty attractive, plays guitar; really smart; kept stepping differently to walk next to me @ 6 flags; xchanged phone #'s; concert w/ him 2mrw; too good 4 me?
 3. –

Taped Fortune Cookie paper:

> You have a charming way with words. Write a letter this week.

wow. I'm on ecstasy Right now. Everything is so surreal. It's like, I just sat around for 4 hours in the TV lounge watching TV and eating m+m's and watching ppl play pingpong and chess. Today's my last day on anything. See, here's the thing. I got extremely high yesterday; smoked like 5 blunts and got completed roasted. The color of the grass was changing from green to light green and everything except me was on like a diagonal axis. Anyways, i was just sitting on this bench and I was thinking about the whole situation w/ my parents. Maybe I am what the whole world sees me as. Maybe I'm a teenager out of control. Like, from inside I see other ppl in much worse situations than myself… like Calvin Dodona for example. He's been thru it all and all his drug use led to 1 thing…Rehab. Being clean again. But anyways where was I … Oh yea …… the people I see in worse situations are at the bottom of the pole. They're not going anywhere and that's fucking depressing. But by using them as a comparison to myself – is that really what I want to be? Even if I don't go through as much, i still don't wanna be like any of the ecstasy users i've ever met. I thought I could get away w/ just smoking pot in high school and controlling my curiosity for other stuff. But everywhere I go i somehow find the drug crowd. Like, fuck, its all coming clear now … what my parents were saying about pot being a gateway drug, what Dr. DeSantos was saying about how careful I have to be if i experiment. Like, I was walking down the street today with "ovadiah" and yada and I just remember thinking "this is my last blunt for a looong time" and i can't wait to be sober again. I'm gonna sell all my weed, or just let ppl smoke it. Then i'l hide away my pipe, for keepsake purposes, and start this new quest for a natural high ("off of life" haha….) And I know I'm gunna hate lookin back at this shit when i'm sober… cuz when i'm not fucked up sometimes I don't know how to interact w/ the rest of the world. 2:08 AM, i'm finally sobering up, but i'm feeling a little frizzed from earlier. I swear I have 2 personalities. One's the volunteer, sober, doctor-aspiring straight A responsible nice young woman. When I'm that girl I want to spend time w/ my mother and just go running and out to eat and spend as much time as i can w/ my parents before I leave for college. But all it takes is 1 thing my parents do and I turn into Amy #2. Amy #2 is the girl that thinks she's being <u>way</u> too overprotected. She freaks out whenever her parents get suspicious, even though she deserves it for continuously disobeying and shattering trust. When I'm that girl I just wanna go out and get really drunk or high. I usualy wanna take a painkiller or something but i mostly don't. (btw, i'm keeping my painkillers just in case). Like i honestly think I can beat my yearning for drugs and shit. When I went through my cutting stage, I used a razor blade religiously to get out my stress. The cuts weren't deep or anything, I just used it as my way to deal w/ frustration. Now i use drugs. and that's why i think i have a problem. Who knows, i might be overreacting but if you think of it this way – i just got caught for doing coke. Like on a random piss test. That's raw fuckin evidence. I'm in the midwest for the month while my parents are fervently searching my room for any trace of drugs or paraphanalia. But do I learn a lesson from that shit? No… since I've been here I've smoked weed over 10x, rolled on 2 xtasy, taken perks, and drank smirnoff + malibu. Wouldn't a controlled person be able to get her act together, like even just until her parents trusted her a little more? I just can't believe it's taken me this long to realize shit. ~~even if I'm not do I've~~ I guess I've just masked shit by thinking of other things. like the hippies – they were a generation of pot smokin, acid trippin doobies. But they turned out okay… i mean their generation hasn't turned to shit right? And then there's the kids i hang out with…. like Audrey…. she tells me how overprotective my mom is (which is totally true) but then she also talks about how the shit we do isn't such a big deal. Tonight though, I was fucking crazy. I was sitting in an armchair in the TV Room and I was just thinking about how everythings so strong on E. I could feel it seeping through my muscles and in my veins. And then my heart started Racing and all i was thinking about was how much I needed some water. Like i was probly overreacting but i was kind of scared i'd pass out or something. Like what if i just passed out in the middle of that floor? They'd prob. hafta call an ambulance and i'd go to the hospital. if my parents found out they'd flip… put me in a detox hospital or something. That'd be so bad. So it's july 4th today and I'm happy i'm still chillin. I'm about to go get some wink and listen to some jams. I'll stay updated on my progress as a sober person. shit i wrote a lot.

      – Amy

July 4th 06'

Hey,

So i got thru my first day being sober. woke up w/ a mad headache and took some advil. That was the most expensive yet one of the best highs i've ever been on. Talked to this girl today (who ppl say is like a crazy ass party animal). [...] Lon's told me Lily's been over his house w/ vincent and then he leaves this comment in her facebook that's like 'ur pic is pretty sexy'. and they both have shit in their profiles w/ no person cited. Like his says ♥ unforgettable * *. I'm guessing the stars mean Lily Jackson b/c he can't actually write her name. I can't believe she'd do that to me. That bitch. Fuck it. I'm doing OK w/ this sober thing. It's the first time i really have to fight the urge to get high. We'll see how it goes.

      – Amy

July 8th

"Party animal". she's fucking cool. i only met her like 4 days ago. Her group calls me "big-tits" Amy. She's from the Pacific Rim and she's the craziest girl ever. She's just so wild she makes out w/ everyone in a given room – guys, girls... maybe that's what i find so interesting about her. She has the self confidence to just go insane w/ chics. I bet she has the most wild sex. We hung out a few times here. I heard about her thru a bunch of ppl... everyone talked about how pretty she was and how fun she was to hang out with. I met her when i was leaving the TV lounge 1 day. She was wearing a CVS name tag that said 'Wahab'. We talked about how we both had weed and then went our separate ways. The next day this guy (my project partner) told me about how my Asian friend almost got kissed by "Party Animal" the night before (apparently "Party Animal" was drunk + hi off her ass). then my Asian friend called me over and told me about how "Party Animal" was like: "who r u" to this other chic... so the girl tells her n shes like "Big tits Amy?". [...] so then that day i saw "Party Animal" walking out of the dining hall and i called her name. so she walked over and talked to me, my project partner + Lawana for a minute. She told me she was getting high after class. I got really shitty drunk that night and ended up passing out @

like 8. The next day i got Really hi; called Paco ("party animal"'s friend) and we planned to meet + smoke after ping pong. Went down to Pacos Room. "party animal" was there. We talked for a little and i gave her a perc [[Percoset, a prescription painkiller]], but i don't think she took it. She took my picture a few times on her camera. We went (me, Paco, "ms. nose ring," "party animal", Tully + "louisiana") and smoked lots of weed using my piece and buttercup. "party animal" linked arms w/ me on the way across the field into the building. When we went back we chilled in Pacos room, listened to some tunes, drank some shit… "party animal" made out w/ this girl Varenka for a good 2 minutes, then had a 3 way kiss w/ Buster + Varenka. I faked falling asleep for a minute and Hobson + "Party Animal" got me up. When she was leaning over me ppl were like "party animal" … don't make out w/ her" and she was like "i'm not going to…" idk tho i think if the opportunity arose we might kiss. We got up and went smoking again when we saw her geek friend (who, as she told me, she had a "geek" crush on). [...] She also told me how it sucked that we <u>just</u> met on her 2nd to last night here. ☹ Then we went upstairs to make popcorn. [...] We got on the discussion of my all girls school and when Buster asked me if i was bi i said no. eventually i left so "party animal" could hit on "Geek". Oh and i can't forget, "party animal" went and got a new key for me when i lost mine. She pretended she was me it was so nice. I saw her again last night. I was just walking around and i went into my project partner's room where my Asian friend, Hobson, "party animal"'s roommates, some chic in a bathrobe, and some other girls + boys were. "Party Animal"'s roommate was so cocked so i helped carry her upstairs. "Party Animal" and her boyfriend were having sex so they locked us out till they got dressed. When I walked in "party animal" was like "oh …. its you!" and she talked to me about how unfortunate the situation was last nite (maybe that we didn't chill for long?). then she started prancing around in her bra + undies. She goes "hey, do you want something to drink?" n i got some bacardi that she had saved in a coke bottle. i went into her room while "Ms. nose ring" was passed out near the bathroom. [...] We decided to go smoke (her, me and Paco). She wasn't gunna smoke but she said she'd keep us company. [...] We got [...] a group of ppl who wanted to go to the court-yard to blaze [[smoke marijuana]] n shit. [...] Then a bunch of us walk[ed] to the stairs to sneak out. Suddenly, "party animal" runs upstairs. [...] Well that was the last I saw of her. I didn't want to call, cuz i didn't want her to think it was sketchy. I didn't see her this morning cuz Lawana and I did…. wake and bake [[inhale marijuana smoke/vapor immediately upon waking up]] @8, my favorite bakery, more smoking @ the park; my favorite bakery sit down. i went thru the book when i got back to the dorm and it had her sign out date recorded. i have her # but it only works in the U.S. and she's probly on her way home rite now. I'm just so sad everyones gone. Mr. Chill West Coast. "Party Animal." Lawana. Pliny. "Louisiana". Shit. I'm so not ready for this emotional loss. I've broken my sobriety promise but that was all for "party animal". cuz I thought maybe she'd notice me if i was under the influence. From now on i'm clean.

Signed,

~~June~~ July 8th

Hey,

So i took a nap and ate lunch and watched tv, went on myspace & facebook in the computer lab and had a long convo w/ my RA [[Resident Assistant]] about how sad we both are that everyone's gone. I found out "party animal" has a myspace. I might ask her to be friends in a week or 2. IDK what it is, i just feel like i have this infatuation w/ her... like the way she lives her life. I really miss the session 1 kids. Like, the new kids are here but it's not the same. I miss the little tingle of anxiety i got whenever i walked down to the 1st floor. I also miss my family. I know I'll be so excited to see the cats + dog. But I'm not looking forward to my parents confrontation. Lab @ 10 AM 2mrw so i gotta run.

♥ Amy

July 20th

LAST DAY in midwest

Holler,

So I'm back from the midwest now. My last few days were pretty fun. I went on a packie [[liquor store]] run w/ this boy who looks like he's 30 on Friday nite. Then [...] a bunch of ppl went to play midnight soccer. When they got back we all went up to Tullys room and started drinking. I only drank beers b/c I wanted to see what it was like being the only sober person. It was actually really interesting. Watching the intoxicated people around me was entertaining. Packie run boy got WASTED and started hitting on me like CRAZY. I really don't like him when he's drunk. The French boy (who i find absolutely adorable) was going craaazy. [...] He had his arm around me for a good part of the night, but in a totally friendly (not sexual) way. This amazingly awesome boy from the mountains was fairly sober. He was like my protecter from all the boys that were trying to get w/ me (mostly packie run boy). I talked to him and this kid from NYC for a lot of the time. This boy from Germany (who's super cute) (and we kinda had a flirty thing going on) was pretty shitty. He kept trying to get me to take shots but i didn't. This other boy was so drunk and he was being hilarious. He was doing this funky dance in his boxers and just being totally cute. [...] This other guy didn't come which kind of upset me. Actually it didn't bother me that much. We kinda had a flirtish thing going on, but it wasn't like I had a crush on him. This probably sounds totally bitchy but I really wanted pictures of us together more than a hook up. So i could post them on facebook and almost gloat about the times i had in the midwest. Maybe it's about Lon. I don't think i have feelings for him anymore but there could be some bottled away. Back to the midwest... So later that night this girl (pretty good looking; apparently into coke) (who Tully was getting really touchy w/ even tho they're both in relationships) was walking around all shitfaced [[drunk or high]] and even tho we've only ever said about 2 words to each other, she suddenly sees me and yells, "Amy!!", then runs up and kisses me on the cheek. Later we went to the girl's room to try to put her to bed. Someone made a speculation that her + Tully were hooking up. We were all standing around her (she was laying on the floor) and she goes "No... the only person i wanna hook up w/ is Amy!". Hahaha. I was flattered but still kinda like uhh... Okay. Anyways, me and "Mountain boy" left after Tully had a bipolar fit and told us to leave. Later i saw the girl <u>again</u> and she ran up and kissed me on the cheek again, claiming she was completely sober. [...] I ended up going to finish my packing @ that point, so i said bye and went to bed. In the morning I said bye to suitemate 2 and packie run boy, found an ipod and left w/ Anya and her husband. And that was that.

---

memories from the midwest

- Taste of the midwest w/ Mr. Chill West Coast
- My favorite bakery croissants, cookies, bday cake ice cream
- Getting Steve'd w/ lawana (last morning)
- Elevator w/ Steve and R.A.'s
- Lawana's farting roommate
- parties in pacos w/ "party animal" + crew
- midnight soccer + walk back w/ suitemate 2 (cookie monster)
- packie run w/ the boy
- Walking around the city alone @ night when trying to find classical concert

– percs + police

- night on ecstasy
- six flags and adventures w/ Pliny

July 20th [2]

So, as i mentioned, i'm back from the midwest. I've been hanging out w/ Calvin a lot.

★ Tuesday
  - met outside Friendly's
  - went to Ground Round and then back to his house; chatted w/ his Mom
  - on way home he goes "idk if Audrey told you, but i like you"
  - i told him i wouldn't discuss my feelings for him as long as he has a g/f

★ Weds
  - he came over in morning; watched Clerks
  - he got out of work early (he just 'didn't feel like being there') and called me to chill
  - picked me up and we went to his house
  - he took shots; got pretty drunk.
  - got really tense: "i really like u… i wanna be w/ you."; tried to kiss me a lot (I didn't let him); "i've wanted u since the moment i seen you"; held hands on way home

★ Thurs (Today) - came over in morning when Mom not home; watched Saved by the Bell
  - Kept touching my leg (but i kept pushing him away)
  - told me he was gunna 'talk to nancy' today; kept saying he knows how he feels and he doesn't want to be w/ nancy
  - called and asked if i wanted to chill @ 9 but i said i couldn't
  - called again and asked if i wanted to stop by his work for free coffee
  - i ended up bringing him ice cream and i got free coffee
  - he said he'd call me when he gets out of work

Do i like him?
  - kind of; i have a little crush
  - but – i'd be totally shunned @ school for 'stealing nancy's man'

---

2. Amy is 17½.

- i'm just gunna let things play out
- i'm @ precalc class rite now so i gtg, but i'll write next time
  I get a chance

♥ Amy

7/22

Holler,

so i'm chillin @ volunteering @ the hospital. calvin wants me to get him a volunteer job here. I saw him yesterday and again 2day. Yesterday we went to Canalboro in the morning and he picked up a bunch of shit.

7/25/06

Rize Rize

(cont. about Sunday)
- met Calvin after volunteering (skipped family picnic).
- went to his house w/ Audrey + her guy friend drank beers (3 got me buzzed); they got some Harry [[heroin]] from Calvin's friend; Calvin offered me a bag but i wouldn't take it; later went out 4 ice cream; $10 went missing; got banana split. talked till like 3 in the morning! nancy + calvin <u>huge</u> fight over Scott - Monday: went to Calvins and got <u>really</u> flirty; grabbed his junk [[heroin]] a few times, cuddled
- later went to my house and played ping-pong
- he didn't smoke a but for like 2 hours; we were having so much sober fun [...]
- basement hug in the dark (so sweet)

Today – picked me up ~ noon
- chilled @ his house; his mom cleaned sooo long in his room. then we went up and went <u>crazy</u>; ton of dry humping etc
- i'm beginning to think Calvin's only a reason to make Lon jealos. i don't even know if i like him, esp. after we hook up. (same way w/ every guy since Edmund;)

maybe i'm afraid boys won't like me after we hook up, so i try to push <u>them</u> away first. thats my theory.
- calvin's called like 8 times since 4... wants to chill w/ me + his friend 2nite. haven't answered. i might tell him i was hanging out w/ an ex boyfriend; maybe start a little jealosy? I'll let u know how it turns out.

♥ Amy

The following letters summarize much of the tension following Amy's return from the midwest.

August 25th, 2006

My dearest mother,

I'm so sorry. I'm sorry for the pain I've made you deal with throughout my life, especially during the past year or so. Sitting at the restaurant this evening I looked over and noticed you smiling. Mom, you have the most kind, warm hearted smile I've ever seen. It reminded me of all the amazing times we've had together...visiting Aunt Hattie, going on the occasional run, driving to school (and of course hitting up Tulips), listening to classic oldies and, of course, laughing about your ever-famous attempts at hitting that mailbox in the town center with the car for the 2nd time. Seeing you smile made me realize how much I want to have our old, fun times back. I *hate* being the source of your unhappiness and pain. I feel like drugs and alcohol have created a barrier between us that goes beyond what I'd ever imagined they could. I had no idea they could be the cause of such a level of distrust and separation. Honestly, mom, I don't feel I have a problem with any recreational substance. As I've said before, sometimes I'll make the wrong decisions simply to fit into the social scene. It seems ridiculous when I say it like that, but I guess that's what my 'deal' is. You know what I've come to realize though? Not even the best high in the world would be worth risking my relationship with you. I find even the least significant times we have together to be 1000x better than any experience I've ever had under the influence. I just wanted you to know that. No matter how many hurtful things I say when I'm angry, I just need you to understand that I love and care about you so much. And as cheesy as this sounds, I wanna be the one to make you smile some day.

I know this letter is barely articulate and far from "perfect", but I thought it was better to get out my feelings this way than waste time thinking of the ideal words. I hope we can work everything out because I want to have an awesome senior year and I want our relationship to flourish during my last year at home. Feel free to reflect on this letter, but please try to keep it between us as best you can.

Love you so much,

Amy

xoxo

August 27, 2006

Dear Mom and Dad,

I read over your letter about driving privileges and I found it relatively sensible. I realize that I've made some mistakes over the past few weeks and I understand that I must pay the consequences. I do, however, have a few suggestions and changes to the "plan" that I'd like you to consider.

First of all, I'd like to talk about the proposed 6 week driving suspension period. As Dr. DeSantos would say, we approach situations involving trust completely differently. I look at most punishments as moving too slowly, while you see them as moving way too quickly. I'm not trying to ask for my driving privileges back right away, because I agree that I do need time to rebuild the trust necessary to regain your confidence when I'm behind the wheel. Believe me, I don't want you guys to have to worry every time I take the car out, and I think waiting a few weeks in exchange for your trust is definitely a fair trade off. I would, however, like to ask you guys to shorten the suspension time to 3 weeks. I think 21 days is a long enough period in which to establish a healthy level of trust, assuming I don't have any more major slip-ups. As you mentioned, getting my license back would also provide ease with regard to transportation; I am, for the second time, looking forward to a point where I don't have to pester you for rides to the mall or to meet up with friends. Let me try to prove my progress and if you're not convinced after 3 weeks you can re-extend the time period. Feel free to talk this over with Dr. DeSantos or Mr. Coolwater.

I have no problem with the proposed property searches because I no longer have anything to hide. I would like to ask that you refrain from reading my diaries and personal notes, or I will stop writing them. I also understand your suspicions about potential drug use on my part. I can honestly say I'm have not used any recreational substances recently, nor do I have the desire to use in the future. To prove this to you, I will agree to random tox-screens, but I'd ask you to stick with urine tests. And no, I'm not asking for this because I want to 'cheat' the system because, whether you believe me or not, I have never used previously bottled urine for my tests. I just feel like blood and hair tests are too invasive. If it makes you feel more comfortable, I know there are systems where a nurse or supervisor actually stands in the room while the subject is taking a urine test to prevent fraud, and I'd be willing to do something like that.

Other than those two points, your proposal sounds fair. Please think about what I've written.

Lots of love,
Amy

Another gap in Amy's journals occurs during the first six months of senior year. Yet her list of "STUFF I DID WHEN I WAS 17" captures her experiences with more substances. The drug counselor she refers to is probably Mr. Coolwater, whom she saw once. At school, Amy continued as cross country co-captain and took on a demanding courseload. She was also vice president of SADD, Students Against Destructive Decisions. After a fight with her classmate Nancy in December, she had to sign a behavioral contract. And she applied to six colleges.

STUFF i DiD WHEN i WAS 17

- First time recieving steve for my birthday
- First positive drug test (coca)
- First potential/almost love
- First experience w/Harry
- First epiphanies: realization that I am actually in trouble
- I lost my mind
- Got into first applied to colleges: UVM + Creighton
- First visit to a drug counselor
- First fistfight

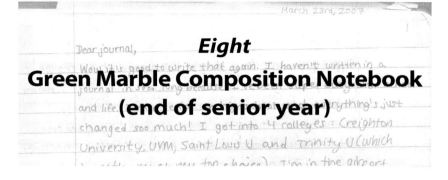

Eight
Green Marble Composition Notebook (end of senior year)

....

Lon wrote the following passage in Amy's journal.

Tuesday, March 20, 2007[1]

[…] You know, you're such an amazing person off drugs. You say you don't really know how to interact with people without some drug influencing you. But the way you are off drugs is so incredible and enjoyable. You don't need anything to change you. You're perfect just how you are. And I'm so happy that you stopped all the other drugs and pills for me, and hopefully somewhat for you. You really don't need them. […]

March 23rd, 2007

Dear journal,

Wow, it's good to write that again. I haven't written in a journal in sooo long because I've been super busy with school and life. I'm a senior in high school and everything's just changed soo much! I got into 4 colleges: Creighton University, UVM, Saint Louis U and Trinity U (which is pretty much my top choice). I'm in the airport right now in Newark, NJ waiting for my flight to Saint Louis. I'm visiting SLU for this 'Admitted Students Day.' It kinda sucks because I have so much to write down about everything that's gone on but I don't have the time or energy to do so. Agh… I'm reading this over and I realize I'm writing so differently than I usually do in journals. ~~because~~ I think it might be because one of my more recent journals was stolen by Alonzo Quetta! Alright, now before you make any judgements about him (like Audrey and her guy

─────────────────────

1. Amy is 18.

friend have…) Alonzo is my current boyfriend and my first love. I'll probably be writing about him a lot in here. But he did steal my journal last weekend because he wanted to see the deepest side of me (which, I'll admit, I've been apprehensive in showing). And how I have this weird, sort of scared feeling that it might happen again some day. Maybe it's a good thing though… I probably should be more careful w/ what I write in here because that wasn't the first time my journal was stolen (my mom stole and read one over the summer). Agh, I kinda hope this feeling goes away because I have so much to say but I feel like I can't open up, even in here. I guess I'll just start off with a daily report. Let's see, I saw Lon yesterday after school. I got my car back! (I crashed it Feb. 2nd and I've been driving my dad's minivan ever since). [...] I've been seeing him so much lately but I haven't gotten bored of him and I don't think he's gotten bored with me. The other night I dropped by his house and we drove to our 'spot" (this little alcove in a cemetery near his house) and we just talked for a little while. We talked a little about summer plans (his dad's making him work at this camp for like a month) and then I got to thinking about after the summer and I got wicked depressed. Then I started crying. crying! For no reason… Well, I guess it was because I realized how much I'm gunna miss him next year when I'm off at college. So we went into the back seat and just cuddled for 15 minutes and told each other how in love we were and I started to realize how much I'd fallen for this boy. Wow, sorry to get so mushy there. I guess i just wanted to show a little piece of how i feel right now. The only problem is, he's opened up to me so much and showed me so much about himself and, unless i'm a total moron, I'm pretty sure that he's honest with me about everything. I've opened up to him about a lot of things but there's still stuff I want to tell him; stuff that I feel guilty keeping from him or lying about. Like, last night he asked me if I've ever gone fake tanning and I know he hates fake girls so i told him that I have in the past but I don't anymore. And then we were talking about my car and he asked me if we bought it new and i told him we bought it with like 13K miles on it, even though i know we got it with 18,000. I don't know why the hell I did that, I sort of just spit the number out. Then, I guess he has an idea about this but not totally… I'm soo flirtatious with other guys. I'd never cheat on him (like make out with someone else or do <u>anything</u> more) but I always flirt with other guys (like old friends) like crazy. Like, Kumasi and I "cuddled" last night just for fun. It was nothing big at all and I felt absolutely nothing sexual. like if you could have less than no feelings for or attraction towards someone;

that'd be my situation w/ Kumasi. We're really good old friends and he's a great guy and we hooked up like sophomore year but him and I both know that friends is all we're gunna be. And I know that's such a sore spot for Lon, my relationship with Ricardo. He thinks so differently of me + Ricardos relationship than we do. But I can totally see where he's coming from. Like, if he went over that freshwoman's house I'd be <u>pissed</u>. And if I found out they were cuddling I'd probably tell him we needed to take a break. Wow, you know what i just realized? I think the reason i can't open up to him is that I don't 100% trust him. Like, I trust him 99.$\overline{9}$ (repeating) % but sometimes I wonder… and like sometimes I go through his cell phone and see texts from other girls or series of text messages that he send but where he's deleted their responses. Wow, I just dropped my orange pen under this kiosk so I'm trying to find a new one that works, haha. But anyways, back to my point. I think the main reason I don't 100% trust him is that I'm scared of getting hurt because I'm so paranoid that he'll get bored of me or fall in love with someone else and leave me in the dust. Wow. I sound like a depressed emo chick or something. But I know that I flirt 50x more than him with other people, even though we both do it for the same reason (maximum attention). And that's probably the reason I don't trust him – because i just assume that he acts the same way as me. So, in conclusion – i have to start getting my shit together and not being such a tease – because I don't want to be at all. But I just feel so much more secure when I have 10 guys flirting with me than just 1. Because that way if one of them hurts me I have 9 backups. See, it has some logic to it! Or not… Okay, so that's going to be one of my new goals. I think it'll also help my social skills – to have good, non-flirtatious boyfriends. [...] I'm waiting for a call from Lon right now. I left him a voicemail that my flight got delayed so hopefully he calls when he gets home from track. It's so good to be this close with someone He's really becoming one of my closer friends. I guess the only problem is I'm starting to grow apart from my other friends. Like, I constantly lie to Audrey – my best friend! – to hang out with Lon when she wants to hang out. I'd wanna hang out with them both but Audrey like despises Alonzo. OK well the airport is getting wicked crowded now and I'm like surrounded by people so I think I'm gunna go shopping now. But I'll probably be writing back sometime soon. Later, journal.

♥ Amy

Saturday March 24th, 2007

Dear Journal,

Today has been so busy! But in a good way ☺ Right now I'm on my plane from Saint Louis to VA then to Manchester. I ended up getting to Saint Louis 6.5 hours late because of those damn thunderstorms. I went right to bed when we got to our hotel. Then this morning I got a voicemail from Lon and he said that he got his license! So I didn't call him back for like an hour because I got sort of depressed and really negative about our relationship. I don't know if it was because I ran out of meds, so I haven't taken my Celexa since Thursday or if I'm just upset in general. Sometimes I just get so moody and paranoid about me and Alonzo. I'd like to think I have things under control but sometimes I just can't get it together. Like I was just thinking about our future and like whether or not him having his license is gunna change us. God, I'm such a bitch. I should've been so happy for him like immediately, but all I could think about was how many more parties he'll be able to go to and how much more attention he'll start getting from people without licenses (especially girls). But now that I write it down I'm realizing that I don't think he'll want to pick up other girls. At least I hope not. I was reading 17 magazine yesterday and it was talking about how if you're paranoid about your current boyfriend because of past relationships, you should try focusing on signs that he loves you and that he's not looking for other girls/cheating on you rather than signs that he is. I think I'll start trusting him more. One of the things I think we have in common is not being totally popular with everyone. Like we both have our groups of friends but ~~we totally~~ I think we both yearn for acceptance by the 'popular' crowd sometimes. And we both care <u>so</u> much about what other people think and what's said about us behind our backs. He's just a little more open about it. I think I need to tell him that I'm the same way. I have so much trouble opening up to him and admitting my insecurities, but I am getting better, Anyways, enough about Alonzo. Let's talk about SLU! I totally fell in love with it. There are so many things about it that attracted me: the gorgeous campus, the closeness to downtown St. Louis, the public transportation, the meal plans, the kindness of all the faculty, the new arena they're building, the student organizations, 'Welcome Week', the location, the bus they have for $1 (so I can visit my sister!) and just so many other things. I bought a ton of clothes from the bookstore and then I bought Alonzo a shot glass from the airport. I wonder if me and him will drink when I get back. I haven't done any drugs or drank since 2 Thursdays ago! Alonzo and I made an agreement to not do anything for a week and we actually followed through. Hold on, i'll write more later!

♥ Amy

Sunday 3/25/07

Dear Diary,

 Absolutely amazing day turned horrible. I started off driving to the bagel store and the Big Box electronics store w/ Lon in his beamer [[BMW]]. I felt so good driving in such a nice car next to my boyfriend. It was like a movie – we would be the couple everyone envied. Then we went to his house and cuddled and watched Criss Angel's magic show and ate easy mac and it was so much fun. We just bonded so much. Then we left the house @ 5 and drove around and laid on this picnic table in a playground and talked and went on the swings. Then we drove to this field and parked and started hooking up like really intensely! But then these lacrosse players totally saw us so we drove away and one of them bowed at Alonzo. So we drove to "our spot" (in the graveyard) and continued where we left off and it was great until Alonzo did something gross for like half a second but i got so upset and felt so violated that I started crying. Then afterwards he felt sooo guilty and wouldn't stop hugging + kissing me and saying sorry and that he loved me. So I was still a little upset when I dropped him off so he brought me out a slice of cake w/a note that said 'i love you' on it. But while he was getting the cake I was looking through his texts and i saw some really disturbing ones like one that said 'hey what did we have to drink' from Tamar, even tho he swore he didn't drink this weekend. Then one before that he sent said something bout hanging out to Tamar then 'i have booze'. Then there were some to Tamar from him that said "i just want to be with you" and "do you want to stay?" and then when she asked why he wrote: "you know why". So I told Alonzo i didn't want to talk to him and drove away. Then i got home my mom told me that Lon's dad had called and Lon was in huge trouble b/c he lied about driving people and about where he went so he called and i answered and he told me [...] his life was going to shit tonight. I guess his dad took away Lons BMW privelages indefinitely and he was sad b/c he knew i hated him. So we talked for a while and then his Dad wanted to talk with him and he said he'd call me back in 10 but he hasn't and I'm so worried that his dad took him to the hospital or something. I've tried calling like 1000 times but no answer. Then I cried really hard for like 15 minutes because I don't know what to do because I'm so angry at him but worried about him @ the same time and there's no way i can reach him. I'll write back tomorrow.

 – Amy

....

Note: Amy is now buried within yards of "our spot." We selected the plot without knowing the significance of this place in her relationship with Lon.

3/26

Lon's fine. Turns out he turned all the lights off and fell asleep last night. We talked a lot today and I'm still upset and a little angry but somehow he managed to justify everything. It's so weird like he does things that look so horrible to everyone and if i saw one of my friends in my position i'd probably be like 'dump his ass'. But everything just seems so different and it's almost like an extraordinary situation with us. I might be a fool but I'm a fool in love.

♥ Amy

p.s. I've decided to make an Amy + Alonzo scrapbook. I'll start brainstorming in the back. Wow i'm a nerd. Since when did 'brainstorming' become part of my vocabulary?

Friday, March 30ᵗʰ 07'

Hellooo Journal,

Finally my week is over! We had no school today so I cleaned my room and watched part of 13 and Pulp Fiction. Then I went over Calvin's and we went to the liquor store and then hung out @ his house and talked a lot to his mom! Then this cute guy (w/ a red beard!) and his g/f and winston came over. Then i left and picked lon up from track practice and we talked about how i flirt too much with guys. Then we went for pizza and talked about ugly people and how your looks kind of decide your place in society. It was a pretty interesting conversation. We also talked about how Rosemary and this other girl remembered me because of my huge nose. That got me kind of sad because my nose is definitely my biggest insecurity. But Alonzo was just so nice about it and he tried reassuring me by saying that like there's nothing i can really do to help it and when you think about it that way it's not a big deal. Cuz it's not like acne or something that i could fix by putting in effort. I was just kind of born this way. We drank some of our Budweiser 40's in the pizza place parking lot. It was the first day we drank since we made our pact not to do any drugs or alcohol for a week (which was 2 weeks and 2 days ago). So we did pretty well with that and for a lot of it i wasn't even craving anything. It's so weird because i remember going for a period of a couple months last year when i didn't do anything just by chance i think. But the difference between then & now is that last year it was so easy to stop everything – i don't think i even questioned my loyalty to the anti-substance thing. But this year it's been such a challenge for me to give up everything. Very interesting. Look how complicated these drugs have made

my life. Anyways then Lon got really upset b/c i was on the phone w/ Audrey and she was talking poo about him and a few other things. So we talked for like an hour and his mom called and forced him to make a decision about whether he was going away over April break. He ended up saying yes. So he'll be gone for 7 out of 9 days of break. I guess that's a good thing in some ways because it will give me some breathing space and I'll get to hang out w/ my friends and maybe even plan a little vacation myself. I guess i'm just a little upset because he gets sooo offended whenever i choose to do something other than hang out with him but here he goes saying yes to a trip that will take away our April vacation together. And he kept saying how he didn't want to leave but he just couldn't turn down the trip b/c it sounded cool and his parents put so much effort into planning it. I guess he has a lot more trust in me than i do in him b/c if i left town for a week i wouldn't be able to enjoy myself because a) i'd be missing him and b) i'd be worried about the things he'd do. But i guess in ret-rospection i'm kinda glad he said yes. April break will be interesting. So the rest of the night was pretty low key, we spent like an hour walking around a high school looking for a tennis ball. I vowed to talk to Audrey about her animosity towards Lon. Then we went to our spot, finished our beers and had sex. Then i dropped him off and he cleaned out my trunk from beer stench and we kissed and i drove off. Oh I forgot to write about Thursday night – let's go back in time, 1 day. [...] Thursday i skipped track practice and then [...] I met up w/ Jemima, Maurann, Sherryl, Mariana and "Red Beard" @ Calvin's and we hung out there and ate pizza and Pancakes (my nickname for Jemima) + I talked to his mom for a while and "Red Beard" tried to force me to smoke out of this huge pipe but then i realized a) I didn't want to smoke and b) I'd be breakin my sober deal w/ Lon so I rejected it. Then me, Pancakes and Maurann went back to Maurann's. Well Maurann and I went to her house and Pancakes and Mariana ran out of gas so we drove to pick her up and this policeman drove up behind us and was being a jerk! Thank God i took the beer out of my car @ Maurann's. When we got back to Maurann's we ate grasshopper ice cream and talked and they drank the beer but i opted out because i was talking to Lon earlier and he made me feel all bad when i talked about drinking for Maurann's b-day and he was like "well, i haven't been craving anything…i like being sober." Anyways, then we went to bed and i slept through physical therapy in the AM and we took Maurann out to breakfast and gave her her present (this really sexy virgin mobile phone) and then i went home. And then my day con-tinued as I said on the first page of this entry. A little confusing but ohh well…
♥Amy

Monday April 2nd, 2007

Hey there,

So I've had a pretty eventful weekend. Saturday morning I slept through track practice (3rd day I skipped so my coach is going to murder me on Monday). So I picked up Lon from his track practice @ 10 and we went to Dunkin Donuts and the bake shoppe. Then we went to the sporting goods store and did something I feel bad about. [...] I stole a sports bra, a pair of under armour shorts and an under armour shirt. They we went to the convenience store and stole some candy. [...] So then we went to Lon's house and watched TV and hooked up in his boiler room and his shower and then his Dad showed up so I had to pretend I'd just dropped Alonzo off and his dad and I had a really nice conversation about colleges and Alonzo's trip and stuff. [...] Then Alonzo and I drove [...] to my house and he played piano while i took a shower (b/c i hadn't showered in like 3 days – i really am getting comfortable with him!!). Then [...] we went to the middle school field to play soccer and we wrestled really competitively (almost too much so). I still felt like he was being a bit cold and not affectionate but I brushed it off and he dropped me at my car and I went babysitting and he went back to his town. I had a really good time babysitting. We played w/ their guinea pigs and watched the Disney Channel and played Guess Who. I found out I was getting out around 10:30 so I told Alonzo and he got really excited and told me to come meet him @ this party near my house. He even went out to the mailbox to check the address! So I went there and it was pretty small, around 20 people (I guess a lot of ppl left) and it was cool cuz when I went in like 3 people were like 'Aaammmyyy!' and I talked with a bunch of his friends and it wasn't awkward or strange at all. [...] One of the huge realizations I made about Lon @ the party was that he isn't the Mr. Popular who i thought he was. [...] It's hard to tell but I almost felt like i was more social and comfortable and happy than he was. He was definitely being super affectionate though and paying tons of attention to me and hugging me and introducing me as his girlfriend ☺ [...] So I'm glad i had a good night! Wow, i just wrote a tonnn [[ton]]! So now i'll write about Sunday. So I woke up around 9 and actually started to do some homework. Then Lon called around 11 and played the meanest April fools' joke ever! He told me he'd heard some stuff about me from a 'reliable' source and he didn't think we should go out anymore. So I started freaking out and i asked what he'd heard and he shouted out "APRIL FOOLS!'. I wanted to murder him. So then he asked me out to lunch so i picked him up at like 1. He was still sort of mellowed out and not totally affectionate but then he told me i looked really nice so that made me happy, to get a compliment instead of a complaint for once. Then he was talking about how his friend said i was the prettiest girl their age (i met him in person the other day)! And Lon said he was bein serious. And apparently Vincent IM'd him the other day and was like 'I like Amy. You guys are good together'. So his friends actually like me, which is cool because I'm like being integrated into his social circle. And we're like becoming a "unit" haha... [...] [W]e had a talk about our relationship on Saturday i think and he was telling me how he hadn't even considered breaking up because not only does he love me but he also doesn't want to put the energy into a break up because "it takes just as much energy as asking someone out". [...] I guess from this weekend I've gained some much needed security about our relationship. I think we're finally making the switch from obsessed, crazy, new couple to matured and settled. Like even though he can be a jerk sometimes or not kiss me every time he looks at me or whatever, I've realized that he <u>does</u> love me deep down. So I'm content with our situation. So after the restaurant we went to the convenience store and stole some candy, then to Dunks where I bought 6 donuts. He wanted to go to the mall but I didn't really feel like it and I also didn't want the extra miles on the car (because my mom's been watching it like a hawk). So we went to his house [...] Then I got some more homework done and passed out so it was a pretty good weekend except I'm really not spending enough time with other friends. Calvin's actually becoming one of my really good friends, not in a friends-with-benefits way! And he was calling me a lot all weekend but i didn't call him back or visit him like i said i would. Also, I've really been neglecting Audrey because she hates when I hang out with Lon so I always avoid her and lie about what I'm doing and stuff. So I think I'm going to call her tonight and try to settle things, try to improve her view of Lon. Because I know she hates him because of some of the asshole things he does and I definitely can't justify them all, but she doesn't realize some of the complex issues he has [...] that justify some of his behavior [...] I know he's a good person inside, he just struggles sometimes. I'm in Calc [[Calculus]] class so I have to go but I'll write later tonight.

♥ Amy

Tuesday, April 3rd, 2007

Dear Journal,

So yesterday was pretty low key. I got to school and Maurann was balling in guidance because her parents [...] took away her car, radio, iPod because she refused to open her door while she was cleaning her room over the weekend.

I know they love her but sometimes I wonder how she puts up with all their b/s. So then I went to all my classes and talked to Jemima a lot about Calvin (she's actually starting to like him!). Then after school I talked to Lon and Calvin (I told him Jemima liked him and it made his day lol). Then i went to track practice and got yelled at by coach for missing 2 practices. Then we voted for team captains (we each put down 3 names) and got dismissed. So I went home and showered and actually worked on some homework! I got kind of antsy because Lon hadn't called after track yet so i called him around 6:45 and we had a short + sweet conversation. Then Audrey came over to watch I Love New York with me (the finale was last night) and I talked to her about how I'd like her to give Lon a chance and stop being so mean. She said she'd try and she sounded semi-sincere, so we'll see if she follows through. […] Anyways, I talked to Alonzo at every commercial break and it was getting sort of redundant but he insisted on not waiting till the end of the show to discuss each segment. Oh yeah and during I Love New York Calvin and Reed Offenbach called and told me to come over! I don't know why but I just got so attracted to the idea that Reed was there – like I really wanted to go. Maybe some part of me is still attracted to the fact that he's probably doing junk. Maybe deep down I still want to do it. But I'm not going to. I've been doing so well with my sober deal with Alonzo. I wasn't as tight with w/ Audrey as I normally am. I think we're growing apart. Goodnight.

♥ Amy

April 6th

Dearest Journal,

Sorry I haven't written in so long! I've been so busy with life again. […] I don't really remember what I did on Tuesday. Ohh ya, well I got in sort of a scuffle with Jemima It was sort of immature and stupid on my part but I was going around school telling everyone about her and Calvin and she was getting upset. I guess she doesn't want Nancy to find out. And I <u>did</u> want Nancy to find out because then Jemima and Nancy would bicker. Maybe it's their friendship that's bothering me. I mean, they're not close anymore but I guess I assumed Pancakes would back off after Nancy attacked me this fall. Ugh. I donno. But I was actually pretty mature about the situation. I saw how upset Jemima looked at the end of the day so I called her and apologized and told her it wouldn't happen again. Oh and I talked to Lon later and he asked me to his prom! I'm just a little nervous because he's really good @ dancing and I don't think he knows I'm horrible! Then i texted Vernon Quemoy because Audrey said he was taking me to [his] prom so he confirmed it. I still haven't told Alonzo about it cause I'm not 100% positive it's gonna happen. But if it does I'll have a prom Friday (Lon's) then Vernons prom Saturday then Graduation on Sunday! Ahhh… But Vernon and I are strictly friends and I think he may be gay. The only other thing I remember is that Alonzo and I had a really really good phone conversation; it was probably 3 hours in total. It's so nice to have good, happy conversations. They usually happen when we haven't been together for like 48 hours and we're both kinda missin each other so we put in that extra effort. That's about all for Tuesday.

Wednesday was really good. It was my last day of school before my 4-day Easter break and i was so relieved to be out of school! It started to snow really heavily right after dismissal and i got so angry when my coach made us run in the snow on the track. I wanted to scream. And man did i give him attitude. And afterwards I went to Calvins (which I didn't tell Alonzo about so i felt kinda bad. Anyways, at Calvin's I had a few sips of Jack + coke but i didn't get a buzz. Calvin was hitting on me like crazy even though i looked like total poo and my hair was curly. I wasn't really into it though. [...] So once I got home I popped in the shower and headed to Alonzos [...] I wrote a book report for him on this novel 'Into the Wild' and he worked on papers [...] I was lying on the couch in his living room and writing the book report. Lon was on his computer just across the room and I looked up and he was just staring at me with this loving gaze. It was so ironic because like minutes before, I was staring @ him and thinking about him and I thought to myself "I bet he never stares at me like this when I'm not looking". But sure enough, he did. [...] Anyways, in non-Alonzo news, I've been getting a lot closer with the girls at school like Genia and Jasmine Piave and Nadine. It's cool how they confide all their troubles with me and actually trust me and like me. I've been turning in all my 4th quarter assignments on time. I want to finish the school year strong. And that was my Wednesday.

Thursday. Thursday was crazy. I woke up around 8 and went to track practice. Then I went home, showered and finished & e-mailed Alonzo's book reports. […] I met up w/ him at like 4 at the pharmacy. In the car we talked about how he still feels that i'm too dominant in our relationship and i'm too 'extraverted' sometimes which makes him more shy + timid. I think he just has this underlying insecurity about being younger than me. He has this vision of just being totally dominant over a girl; I think he thinks that's

what he wants. To just have complete power over someone. But I don't know if he could handle it. But i guess I'll give him a little more control. So Alonzo and I drove to Broton and did some shopping; I tried on all these prom dresses and Alonzo critiqued them. Then we met up w/ Jemima & Maurann and went to Calvins. I met his son and his baby's mother there and then Winston and Letitia came over and they were so ripped. They asked Lon and I if we wanted to blaze and we said yes but then kind of avoided it; I don't think either of us really wanted to. We gave Winston and Letitia money to go to the liquor store and got a 12 pack of Budweiser. Then we hung out w/ just me, Lon, Calvin, Maurann and Jemima and drank some beer and talked [...] Then Alonzo and I left and went back to his house. Oh yeah, he also taught me how to play drums a little bit and it was sooo fun. Then [we went to] this party [...] and stopped near the commuter rail because there were a ton of cars there [...] So Lon told me to go say hi to Kumasi who was in one of the cars and i did and I don't know what came over me. Maybe it was the buzz i was getting from the beer or just me being super nervous but I was totally flirtatious with all these boys like Jacques and Grady and Norman and when Alonzo walked over I didn't really embrace him. I just like touched his arm and continued talking with all the guys, barely even acknowledging he was there. It probably would've been a bit much to like smother him with a hug and a kiss in front of everyone but at least I could have introduced him as my boyfriend or something. I didn't even realize what I was doing or how bitchy I was bein until we were walking away and he just got so sad and we had a huge talk about everything and it went back to how I act differently in front of other people and I felt so bad. Then we drove [...] back to Lon's house. There we cuddled and watched this show called "real sex" [...] Then I had to take off so I went home and Lon stared at me while I was walking to my car and kept watching me until i drove away. So Thursday was alright overall. I am just so lucky to be in such an amazing relationship. I know it won't last forever but right now things between me and Alonzo are not far from perfect. I can't wait for prom with my baby boy.
– AMELIA

Friday was interesting: I woke up pretty early to go to physical therapy but they rejected me because my doctors orders were a year and a half old. So my mom and I got breakfast and Alonzo called at like 9:15 to invite me over. So we drove home and I packed for my grandparents' and show-ered and wrote Lon this letter because I still felt bad about the situation from Thursday. Then I went to his house [...] [W]e had the whole house to ourselves for a while so we [...] fooled around on his bed for a few minutes [...] And you know what else i was thinking? It's so nice to just be able to go and hook up with someone, like I don't have to primp myself up or flirt extra hard or worry about being "too easy" because i'm in a relationship. Having a boyfriend is really amazing ♥. So then Alonzo took a shower and his house sitter came when he was in there and i ended up hiding in his dads closet for a couple minutes. Then i wanted to eat so i tried to make cookies and pasta but Lon got pissed (I think it was jokingly but partially serious) and he was talking about how he wanted me to wait because i couldn't have everything right when i wanted it. And then i started getting out the pans and pasta despite what he said and he got mad and kicked me super hard in the leg. [...] [I]t [...] scared me a little so i went downstairs for a while partially b/c he told me we wouldn't eat till i retreated and also cuz i wanted a little space from him. So i practiced drums for a little while and cleaned up the TV area and he called me to come back up like 3 or 4 times before i actually did. Then he was being pretty affectionate again and he baked the cookies and made us spaghetti w/ pesto and put on all this really groovy music and we both kind of sang and danced for a little while and i asked him to make me a mix CD so he did. Then i had to leave so i gave him his easter present (i hid it on his bed under his stuffed animal b/c that way he wouldn't find it / open it till later and it'd be a nice surprise. Then i got my mix CD (he wrote: 'Amelia's Mix ♥ From Alonzo" on it) and i hugged him and took off. Then i went to the grocery store, the vet to get cat food, and home. My mom and i got all our stuff together and my dad drove us to the airport. Then we took off. We ate pizza for dinner at like 10:30 and I talked to Alonzo about his night. And apparently he hung out @ this girl Gudren's house with a bunch of people then went for fast food. I got a little jealous and you could tell by the tone of my voice, but i can't help it. I guess I'm just scared he'll get blown away by one of these RPHS girls and leave me in the dust. That's all for Friday.

-Amy

4-7-07

Dear journal,

Finally i'm caught up with all my entries! Today is Saturday and I'm laying on my bed at my grandparents' next to my sister. For the past like ¾ hours I've been going absolutely crazy. I guess I've calmed down since before but I can't even describe what i was feeling earlier. Lon's at a dance tonight that like everyone from RPHS is going to. Alonzo and i agreed that he wouldn't slow dance with anyone and he wouldn't dance with his ex. But i'm hoping he doesn't dance w/ Lisette (b/c he used to have a crush on her, like right before we had our "thing") or Gudren (b/c he was talking today about how cool she is and how i should get to know her more). So all night I've just been picturing my boyfriend dancing with other girls and it's like breaking my heart. Like i do trust him but what if some girl from a different school thinks he's really cute and he only dances with her all night and they bond and get each others contact info and start chatting? Wow. I think i'm being way too paranoid. well i hope so. He hasn't really texted me all night so he must be pretty busy @ the dance. Okay well i'm going to stop writing before i go insane but i'll write again soon.

> – Ameliaaa
>   Carusooo

4/15/07

Hey Journal,

So it's been a pretty long and hard week. Lon and I haven't been so good. He danced with Lisette at the dance and then got "confused" about his commitment to me. The vibe just completely changed and things have just been so rocky. I really hope we'll pull through this. We went to each others therapy sessions and then Alonzo left for vacation on Friday. It's Sunday now and I've been doin okay with him gone. We've had some pretty good phone calls and I've hung out with my other friends – Friday I met up w/ Jemima and Maurann and we went to ihop with Byron. Then on Saturday I went jewelry shoppin w/ Audrey. Then I met up w/ pancakes and we hung out @ this kid's house in Canalboro w/ his g/f and Audrey's ex (who is lookin sooo sexy!). Then we went to the apartment and I drank a beer and watched everyone take hits out of this 6 foot bong! Oh and I was offered coke [...] but I rejected it. I really think I'm done with drugs especially with Alonzo gone. I've had a lot of time to reflect on stuff and I've been getting so bored just sitting around with people (even like Audrey) and doin the same thing. I'd so much rather play basketball or make a scrapbook or play ping pong or something. Ugh, maybe I'm being too judgemental or hypocritical. But tonight I blew off goin to the movies and sleeping over Audrey's to sit home and play ping pong w/ my dad and jam on the piano and paint my nails and watch TV. I bought prom tix [[tickets]] on Friday! Can't wait. Gotta go watch the I♥NY reunion. Write later!

~Amy

April 16th, 2007

Dear Journal,

Today is my 1 month anniversary with Alonzo! I guess things have been better, maybe a little. We talked on the phone today after he called like 4 times and left a voicemail last night. Haven't heard from him since like 2:30 though. I went out to my favorite Mexican restaurant with Audrey and Sally tonight, then drove around and talked and listened to music and danced. Now I'm just lying in bed watching the office and chillin out and thinkin about Lon. I'm kinda tired so goodnight!

~Amy

4-21-07

Hey there,

Very interesting day. Got interrogated with Alonzo in his BMW by these 2 cops in 2 different towns and we got away with everything. I might elaborate later but now I'm too tired. Also, I read through his texts really briefly and sneakily and saw texts to 2 other girls […] Anyways, I missed Alonzo so much when he was gone but now that he's back I've started to realize the truth about our situation. Do you think it's possible, journal, to love someone for who they used to be but to not love the person they've become? Why did I ask, I'm quite certain it's possible and applicable to my situation. But what am I supposed to do? I feel like it's so hard to let go because I want so badly to dig down and find the old Alonzo somewhere in there. And how am I supposed to know if it's a lost cause? I think me and Alonzo are coming to an end. I don't feel the "sparks" anymore and I think it's because of the lack of any effort on his part. I'm just sick of this emotional rollercoaster he's taken me on and all this pain. I don't know what my purpose of breaking up w/ him would be. I feel like I'd secretly want him to come to me the next day with a big bouquet of roses and tell me how sorry he was and ask me out again. But idk, i might actually break up with him after prom. ☹ we'll see.

♥ Amy

Monday, April 22nd, 2007

Dear journal,

Vacation is over! I didn't get any schoolwork done but I really enjoyed relaxing. Yesterday I went to Lons soccer game and then went out to ice cream w/ him and Vincent. Then we laid on the matts and watched the girls soccer game [...] I took some ativan b/c i was really upset yesterday about Lon stuff, so the day seemed to go pretty well and smooth. We kissed a lot and then "ate lunch" then I dropped him home. I don't know what to do about him b/c i can't imagine not being in a relationship but sometimes i just look at us and know that we're both unhappy. I guess I'll wait till after prom and then we'll have a deep conversation about where we're going. I gtg cuz i'm in French class but I'll write later.

     ♥ ♥ Amy

4/24/07

Everything's changing. I'm finally realizing that love isn't forever. And I feel so naïve. The thing is, neither of us want it to change. Alonzo wants to love me just as much as I want him to, but he can't force it and he can't figure out his feelings. It just sucks because he's the first guy I ever let into my heart and my soul and like some of the deepest parts of me. From the beginning I was soo skeptical and hesitant because I didn't want to rush into things emotionally and I just had a feeling that I should hold back. But Alonzo just kept telling me that I needed to trust him and that he'd <u>never</u> stop loving me. So I trusted him. And I'm so happy that through our relationship I learned to let my guard down and be in a relationship and risk getting my heart shattered so I could have it. And it's not his fault that his feelings for me are changing because you can't control your feelings. I've never seen him like this. And he feels absolutely horrible to the point where he doesn't even want to talk about it because he doesn't want to hurt my feelings. I just watched this episode of House and it had this really good quote which kind of explains my situation. "Once you're the focus of that much attention you become addicted". I'm literally addicted to this relationship and it sounds so fucked up but that's how it is. It's like I had my "high" (when Alonzo was just so obsessed with me) and now I want it back and I'm trying everything to do it. It's a lot more complex but I don't have time to explain. I'll write back sometime. Prom in 3 days.

     ♥ Amy

May 5th

Heyy,

Happy Cinquo de Maio! I'm babysitting right now and we're watching the sweet life of Zach and Cody. A ton has happened in the past few weeks. First of all, I think the reason I haven't been writing is...well 2 main reasons. first and foremost things between me and Alonzo haven't been totally spectacular. I mean we had this really bad slump where I was depressed and crying like every day for about 2 weeks because it just seemed like everything we'd worked up to had gone to crap. And things definitely aren't like they used to be but we're both kinda dealing and as i said last night to him, the good doesn't outweigh the bad right now so we're probably not ~~going to break up~~ make any permanent decisions yet. And even if taking a break would be the best thing, I don't think either of us has the balls to actually do it. As for other parts of my life, things with Audrey are pretty bad. I just keep blowing her off to do stuff with Lon or with myself. I know i need to make more time for my friends and my family but I can't seem to get myself to change anything. I just don't have very much time right now. And I'm really not a bad person but that's the way it must be coming off that way to everyone. Well, except Lon. Oh yea, I also decided on a college. I'm going to SLU! I haven't told the boy yet but I will soon. Oh yea and I had prom! I showed up completely wasted which i now regret because first of all, i don't remember much, second i didn't get to dance very much and the teachers were all suspicious and Alonzo had to take care of me all night. But everyone was babying me and taking pictures with me and looking out for me, and i got so much attention. Even from people i usually don't hang out with. And omg, Alonzo talked to Nancy and told her that he thought me + her should stop fighting. And apparently she said i'm a "good girl" but i "hooked up w/ her boyfriend when i knew they were going out for 2 years". And then after prom we went to Audrey's hotel room and hung out. So Alonzo and i definitely haven't been getting along like we used to but we've been hanging out more than ever. And last week (the Sunday after prom) we went for ice cream and we were actually kind of acting nice to each other and flirty and stuff and things were pretty good for the first time in a while. But then he started being a jerk and eating all the sprinkles of my ice cream that I paid for. So i punched him in the face and then he backed out of the parking lot and hit this car. And it was only a little dent but it turned out to be $890 and so right afterwards Lon went into crisis mode [...] and it was really freaking me out.

5/18
Friday

Went to Alonzo's prom tonight. And I had an unexpectedly good time! I've literally been dreading it for months and up until a few days ago i had it set in my head that i wasn't going, for a few reasons. 1 – i was scared to see all the people i knew from middle school, because i left on bad terms with a lot of people. Then i was also scared to fast dance because i wasn't sure if i'd be up to Alonzo's standards or if i'd look like a total fool. But we went and I got along really well with everyone and had a ton of really good "Hey! How have you been?!"'s with old classmates. And i don't think my dancing was too atrocious either. I ended up dancing w/ Lon, Zeke, Vincent and this guy who was pretty cute. And Lon and i had a pretty good night overall… i think we got some good talking in. […]Oh yea, and three kids got busted for having alcohol so I feel pretty bad for them. But i have a pretty big weekend ahead of me: MVC [[track]] meet tomorrow, the prom with Vernon in the evening, then graduation + helenas party Sunday. I'll write soon!

♥ Amy
P.S. I got a job @ the bagel shop! Wahoo..!

5/21
Monday

Dear journal –
Hey! So I had a really busy weekend. On Saturday I went to get my hair done, then I went to Audreys and we got ready and

Jun. 5th 07

Haha, wowww…

I keep starting journal entries and not finishing. I think its partially because I'm so busy and partially because things aren't as perfect as they once were and when I write I actually have to think about my life. I'm babysitting for this family down the street right now. It was such a long day. I had work 7-1 and drums 2-2:30 and now I'm here from 3-8. So I'll do a quick recap of what's gone on in the time i've been avoiding journal entries. I graduated, I went to Lons prom & my prom & Vernon's prom. I got a job at the bagel store and I'm working there pretty constantly (between 30 and 40 hours a week). I got my report card and it turns out I failed 2 classes (Lit & Bio). So my parents are pretty angry about that or not so much angry as disappointed. And then there's my situation with Lon. I could fill every page in this journal with stuff about him because our situation is just so complex. We're still going out and we're going on 3 months. We still haven't broken up and I have a feeling we won't until the end of the summer when we won't really have a choice. I think our situation is just stale right now. [...] [W] e went on this like month long streak where every single day i convinced myself I was going to break up with him. And i actually brought it up to him twice. But no matter how confident i was when i said "maybe we should break up" or "i think it is time to break up", somehow i'd get this horrible feeling and either we'd talk it out or he'd convince me that it wasn't the time yet. And then sometimes he'd bring it up the next day and be like "well, you're the one that wanted to break up with me". And then at one point I realized that no matter how much one or both of us wants to break up it's not going to happen. Partially because we'd miss each other / be really lonely because right now we spend about 90% of our social time together. And partially because we're both afraid of change. And partially because deep down i think we both feel like there's a really strong connection or at least the potential for one beyond all the bullshit. And we have so many memories together and a break up would just be so painful and draining. Sometimes i want to break up so bad. Like when we've spent too much time together and we get in stupid arguments and he says things that just really hurt me. Like when he calls me an idiot and when he constantly criticizes the way i talk, the things i say, my actions etc. And i know he doesn't but sometimes i feel like he just hates me. And that makes me hate myself. But its not his fault because he just interprets the things i do and say so deeply. Much too deeply. And often incorrectly. And then he gets hurt because of his interpretations of things and when i try to tell him he's wrong he gets even more hurt and acts even meaner, then i get more upset and its just a big cycle. And i'm not even going to get into the conversation we had when he outright told me he was smarter than me about a lot of things and that's why arguing w/ me is so pointless. Argh this is making me angry. But i'm so indecisive and my moods change. For example, when we haven't seen each other in a while i start to really miss him and I just want to hold him and tell him how much i love him [...] I also love social situations with him and his friends. Because of Lon I've like integrated myself back into RPHS society. And I've met so many cool people that I just admire so much because they're all so witty and talented. And they're all going somewhere in life. And they're not drug addicts. I just love hanging out with that crowd. I also love talking about him to everyone. Even like kids I babysit for. And my drum teacher. I just love that he's such a huge part of my life. Alright so that was my catch up on Lon. Now for my catch up on me. There's not much to say except I'm sort of in a hard spot right now. I want to be moving forward psychologically and emotionally and intellectually but i feel like i have so many burdens that are holding me back. Maybe it's my overload of work (w/ babysitting and the bagel store). Or maybe it's my commitment to lon b/c i think about him way more than i think about me). But i just want to progress this summer. I need to figure out how I'm also going to try to write a daily entry because now that I updated you on my situation i don't feel that much pressure about writing so much. I'm about to finish babysitting so i'm going to go home, shower, call Lon, lie in bed and hopefully get some good sleep. Bye for now.

♥ Amy

June 6th
Wednesday

Hey,

I'm babysitting again. Last night I went home and went on facebook and called Lon. He was out tux shopping for RPHS senior prom which is tomorrow. He's going with one of his friends from a while back. I don't know much about her but I've seen her a couple times. She's alright looking; nothing too special. She asked him through a text message last week because she couldn't find a date. I'm a little jealous and uneasy and maybe a bit mad about him going but I guess I can't be too dramatic about it because I did go to a prom with Vernon. I guess I'm just scared because the last time he went to a dance without me (when i went to my grandparents') he danced with a ton of other girls and he came out of it wondering if he could really commit to someone long term. Like dances are almost a little taste of freedom and being single. And i hope he doesn't go to a crazy after party and like get trashed. I guess all I can do is trust him and believe that he'll tell me if anything bad happens. Because being honest is more than just not telling lies. Haha, wow… Anyways he called me back later and i was sort of half asleep so we had a pretty boring conversation. Well it wasn't so much boring as it was irritating because he just didn't seem very focused or interested in talking to me. But he never said he had to go which i was sort of anticipating so i told him i was going to bed and hung up. Then i fell asleep, woke up around 7 and went to work. It was so busy in the morning and in the afternoon this guy Kenny came in and greeted me with "hey cutie". Kenny is this amazingly attractive 45 year old man; sort of George Clooney-ish. He comes into the bagel store just about every week day and every time he literally brings a different girl. It's insane.. And they're all gorgeous and I don't know the full story so I probably shouldn't speculate but he has to be dating at least 5 of them. I wonder how they don't know about each other. You'd think that one day he'd be at the bagel store with Girl #1 and Girl #2 would be craving a bagel so she'd walk in and see him. [...] Anyways, he was chatting it up w/ my manager for a while and they kept looking over at me and later my manager told me that Kenny said I reminded him of one of his ex girlfriends! The guy is really cute but I kind of get a weird feeling whenever I'm around him. So then I took a bunch of food from work and went home and laid in the sun and hung out until 3 when I went to the town school to pick up the boys and their friend for babysitting. For the time I was there and the drive back to their house I was just overtaken by this sad feeling. I was watching the kids from all the grades (K-8) and remembering my time as a student there. And feeling like I'd just blinked the last 7 years by. I'm just growing up so fast and I know I'm not trying my best at life. I wish I could go back in time for so many reasons. Blah this is getting depressing. I'm going out tonight and then leaving for the midwest tomorrow so I'll be so busy! But I'll try to write again as soon as i can.

   Byebye,

                    Amy

                                   June 8th 07
                                   Friday

Dear journal,
Guten Morgen! I'm in the midwest right now for my brother's graduation. After my last entry I left babysitting and went home, then went to the mall to get a new phone (because my old one was slowly dying). Then I went to see Lon and we were both really cranky so we spent a lot of time bickering [...] he doesn't think I appreciate him / respect his talent / give him praise as much as a younger girl might. That kind of went back to the whole me being dominant / older thing. Then he mentioned how we're so similar in so many ways and that's probably why we fight so much. Then, the point I thought the most about – he told me that he doesn't think I know who I am yet. And he explained now he knows who he is and it'd be nice to date someone who was more stable and confident about who she was, even if she

didn't have confidence about much else. And I thought about this a lot and I came to the conclusion that I do know who I am at my core. The reason I seem to change so much is that i'm panicking to change certain things about myself and try out new things. Or maybe I'm fooling myself. Maybe I'm not totally sure who I am sometimes because I have 2 distinct, different personalities. At least I used to. Because I don't like some things about my personality. Like how I lie a lot and how I blow off my friends and family a lot and don't really put effort into building relationships (except for my relationship w/ Lon). so then Lon + I went to for ice cream and then I dropped Lon off And usually I'd be super upset leaving things on such rocky terms with him but for some reason I was really at peace with everything. I called Jemima + Mariana and met up with them and their friends [...] I called Lon on my way home and he wanted me to come see him so he could show me a surprise he made. I told him I'd come as long as we didn't bicker. So I drove to this spot we've been using on a cul-de-sac behind his house. We hung out and he showed me the "surprise": a piece of rope cut and crafted and carefully worked into a rope ladder! He made it so it'd be easier for him to sneak into my house and I made him pinky swear that he'd come sneak in and visit me as soon as he got out of school. Then I went home and slept. The next morning I worked until 10:30 then went home to shower and pack for the midwest. Then i drove to catch the 1:50 commuter rail and on the way I met up w/ Alonzo at his school outside the rec center just to say goodbye and kiss him before I left. So I went off to the midwest and went to dinner at this mediterranian restaurant with my dad, Anya and her younger son. And Alonzo was at senior prom but surprisingly I wasn't obsessing over it all night; I was just kind of having a good time not thinking about him dancing with other girls. I got little jealous flashes but i was able to block them out for the most part. So then we went back to Anyas and I helped her younger son set up his facebook account [...] So that was my Thursday.

– Amy

June 12th Tuesday

Hey,

So as I said earlier, I wento [[went to]] the midwest this weekend! Friday morning I woke up and walked down to my favorite bakery with Anya's younger son and we ate breakfast in a park near their house. Then we went back and my Dad drove me to my sister's apartment. [...]. I went on [her] computer while she and my Dad did some shopping and I found out that

Lisette's boyfriend (a really popular/smart boy from RPHS) is going to Trinity University next year! I was so frustrated and upset at first because one of the reasons I didn't choose Trinity was that I didn't think anybody from around here would know what it is despite it's greatness. I was thinking impulsively and almost sent an email to Trinity asking to retake me as an enrolled student. I thought about it for a while though and I decided that college is about me, and SLU is the best fit for me right now. I'm thinking about transferring to Wash U in Saint Louis if SLU doesn't work out. Anyways, I finally talked to Lon about prom and it seems like he had a good time. I'm really proud of him because he didn't drink at all. So then my sister and I went to the beach (after I took a nap) and we talked for a while. She's [...] an amazing person. then her and I went back to her apartment and showered before we headed out to dinner w/ her Friends @ a pub, then to an Albert Hammond Jr. concert at this really neat venue. Afterwards we went to a small party for this guy's 21st birthday [for about an hour] but I spent a lot of the time on the phone with Lon So then [we] went to her friends apartment and hung out with some people there. They tried to get me to take an ice bong hit but I didn't. So that was my Friday. We woke up really early Saturday morning and took the train to my favorite bakery and met up with my brother's friend, then walked over to graduation. The ceremony was really long but I'm glad I went and I'm proud of my brother. Afterwards we went to this reception at my brothers frat house and I talked to a lot of cute frat brothers. My sister and I went to my favorite bakery w/ my two cousins to get milkshakes. We got back and hung out for a while and [...] (who all my brothers friends pretty much love) got tipsy, which was hilarious. We all walked to Anya's house for yet another reception. I talked to her two sons a lot there until we went to dinner @ with everyone. The younger son insisted on sitting next to me and actually moved my sisters purse to do so! I'm not going to get into that...Anyways I had a good time with everyone and it was definitely a change of scenery that i needed. I also finally started getting close to my brothers girlfriend and friend [...] Oh yea, on the walk to the train from the restaurant this <u>really</u> cute guy was walking out of a store and he saw me and said "Hey sweetheart" in a really cute, not so sketchy way. So that made me feel pretty good. I saw him looking back at us and I had half a mind to talk to him but I was tired and I didn't want to ruin the moment. Plus I have a boyfriend. Sunday, my sister and I woke up and went shopping at some neat stores. Then we went downtown and saw a ton of really cute dogs at various points along the main drag (they were part of this adoption agencies awareness thing. After that we met up with my brother, my two cousins and other aunt at the rooftop grill. Then my Dad picked us up and we all went to the airport. I didn't get home until about 11 and I missed lots of graduation parties. But overall I enjoyed my weekend. Monday I worked until 2 then hung out w/ Lon at my house for like an hour while my parents weren't home. Then I met my mom, Mrs. Guicona, Sherryl and her mom for Mexican food up in the boonies of New Hampshire. Today (Tuesday) I went to work and drum lesson. I'm really starting to like drums especially as I'm getting more difficult pieces to work on. I didn't hang out with Alonzo because there wasn't time. I babysat after. Alright well I'm going to catch some sleep.

    xox

        Amy

Friday June 15th, 2007

Dear Journal,

I can't believe it. Lon and I broke up. It was obvious that things were winding down but I'm kind of surprised it's actually over. Here's how it went. After school Lon called me and we decided to get together and hang out. When I got to his house he seemed super depressed and he said he was stressed about school and just depressed. I pryed until he told me there was other stuff bothering him and then I pryed even more until finally he explained that he didn't know where our relationship was going and asked me what I wanted to do. We talked for about half an hour about all our different options (i.e. taking a break, breaking up, being friends w/ or w/out benefits) and we both didn't know what we wanted. Finally we walked outside into the front yard because I had to go babysitting. We talked for about 5 more minutes and Lon repeatedly asked me what I wanted to do. He said he wanted to agree on a decision before I left and as scared as I was, I knew it had to be done. I told him that we should just be friends and he asked me if I was sure about 100 times. I think he felt like it was something I really didn't want. ☹ In the minutes after we agreed to break up we had the best time we've had in weeks. We just looked at each other and laughed about stupid little things and watched Lon's neighbor run around. We were being really nice to each other but not in a fake way at all. Then Lon gave me an amazing hug that lasted a few long seconds, until I pulled away. He asked me when we'd talk next and I had to pause and fight back tears for a few seconds before I told him to call me tomorrow. I felt like I might actually start crying so I tried to cut the conversation short. I got in my car and turned my head so he couldn't see my face. We looked at each other once more before I put my keys in the ignition and backed out of his driveway. He was watching me the entire time and we waved to each other as I drove out of his road. I didn't really listen to music in the car but I cried a little bit, then called Audrey and cried a little more. I think I just need to accept the fact that it's finally over. A breakup was something I'd been planning but didn't have the strength to carry out for weeks (maybe months) beforehand. Anyways, I went to babysit and i was upstairs watching the kids build forts when I received a text from Lon that said: "I don't know if this is right or wrong :-/". So now I'm just sitting in the kitchen watching Spongebob. I'll write later if I have the energy.

   – Amy

June 26, 07

Dear diary,

My aunt has breast cancer. My dad told me today when Audrey + Lon were over my house. I just got home from Aldens and had a really good talk w/ my Dad about how he's dealing w/ it and how i'm gonna try to spend more time w/ her. She's going in for surgery to-morrow to get the cancer removed. I hope it works. Other than that news I had a pretty great night. I went to a bonfire at Aldens and there were so many ppl there and everyone was pretty nice. And I saw this guy Lester Ufa who i kinda knew in middle school and he's really cute. And we just had so much chemistry and we talked for a pretty long time together. He told me a few times that we should hang out more over the summer. And just before he left he asked for my number but I said no because (1) he has a girlfriend (2) Alden was sitting right next to me and that would have been really inconsiderate of me and (3) I was sort of working the hard-to-get thing. Anyways, I kissed Alden last night for the first time. We made out for a while after going to the beach all day. He leaves for Mexico Thursday though so I'll be without him for a bit. I'm soooo tired. Adios.

   ♥ Amy

Jun 30 07'

Oh the things i do when i'm drunk… Alden's been in Cancun since thursday and he sent me this really nice text before his plane took off. I've been having so much fun w/ Alden and his crowd. We went to this boy's house on Weds. night and i was just a social butterfly and it felt so good. And Alden and i sort of have a "thing" together but I've been keeping it from Lon. I hung out w/ Lon tonight @ his godparents house after i saw ratatouille w/ my dad. Lon and i still have a connection i think but neither of us want a relationship. I got home about an hour late b/c me and Lon were busy hookin up lol. Mom and Dad were pissed,

    – Amy

Wait. Also, Alonzo + I made out so much all night. It was cute. Yesterday I found out some very bad news. Edmund (my ex boyfriend) died in a car accident Thursday night. I almost cried when Audrey told me (she came into my work). I just can't believe he's gone. I can't stop thinking about his Mom and his brother and his girlfriend. They must be so devastated. Death sucks. Agh, i'm tired i'll write more later.
– Amy

Dear Journal,
Tonight was really fun. I went to Lon's godparents house to help him clean up from last night and it was sort of awkward between us. I have a feeling we're going to be each other's occasional nights of sexual pleasure for a little while. And then I went to this kid Lester Ufa's house and we watched Da Ali G show for a bit. Lester is one of the coolest people i've met this summer. Our conversations just run so smoothly and we seem to "click" on a lot of things. I guess it's a little flirtatious but strangely our relationship isn't sexual. I kind of feel like over time Lester could turn into one of my best friends. We just sort of understand each other, even though we've only really hung out a couple times. So me + Lester went to grab a bite and we met Audrey at the pizza place. Then we went to Chili's for dessert. And the 3 of us just bonded a lot and joked around and talked as if we'd been friends for years. It was really cool. Lester has a really overprotective girlfriend who he's madly in love with and we talked about her a lot. And when i got home i had a message from her on facebook telling me 2 back off her man. Then i got another 1 apologizing for the first one. Oh, freshmen…Anyways lester and i are gonna hang out tomorrow after I work and I'm gonna help him pick out flowers for his girlfriend (who'se coming home tomorrow). Oh yea, tonight Lester + I talked on the phone and he told me how he explained to his g/f how even tho we'd only been friends for a few days he considered us good friends now. And he said he shared a lot w/ me. That made me feel kinda special.

    Adios. –Amy

Weds, July 4th 07'

Dear journal,

What a fabulous week it's been! I've gone out every night for who knows how long and summer's just been going great. I went to a bonfire at Mikhail Vahs on Monday with Audrey and we just sat around and played kings and listen to these kids play guitar. Then this other guy, Monty and Mikhail tried to pick us up later. They drove over to my house with a ladder haha…but we ended up bailing because we were so tired. Then yesterday I hung out with Audrey and we met up w/ Mikhail and went out to dinner. Then we drove to this boy's open house. I had so much fun there and I saw so many people from middle school, like Lucian, Rupert, Monty. And everyone was really nice to me. I made a lot of new friends too like this boy who's really cute. We talked a little bit and later (when I was pretty gone) he helped me clean off my really nasty bloody foot after i stepped on a nail in the bathroom. I gave him a big hug goodbye when we were leaving and I walked in on him in the bathroom just before I took off (which somehow resulted in me giving him my number). I also talked a lot w/ Monty about Lon's ex and Lon and Lon's iPod…and Monty's ex-girlfriends. And I walked around with this gay guy who i absolutely love. So overall I had a pretty good night. I feel really bad though because I blew off Lon 2 nights in a row. Yesterday he actually talked to me about how it hurt that I was getting over him so fast, or something along those lines. I saw him for a bit before I went to dinner and when we were parting ways we hugged for longer than usual. And then i was going to visit him after the party but his dad saw my car in their circle so i had to go. But i think he's starting to realize i'm OK without him and that's scaring him. But the truth is i am getting over him and i'm really content w/ life right now. I still care about him and i like don't want him being with other girls and stuff but he's becoming less of a concern i guess. Alright well i'm gonna go take a nap then party it up for the holiday … talk 2 u soon!
     - Amy

Fri, Jun 6th 07 [[really July]]

Dear journal,

Ahhh! Such an intense night. I went out to dinner with my family b/c my brother's leaving tomorrow for D.C. So then I went to meet up w/ Alden and his crowd @ his friend's house (he was having a huge party). [...] The craziness began when I was filling up a water bottle for this girl when I saw this kid jump through the window in front of me into the sink. Then i heard someone say the cops were there so I went down into the basement and followed a few kids into the garage. After about 5 of us went into the garage this guy told someone to lock the door so no one else could come in. We hid in the garage for a good 15 minutes and watched this lady cop at the front door. When she went inside we opened the garage door and bolted. This other kid and I walked thru the woods and fields for over an hour just hiding. I got so scratched up on my arms and legs from all the branches and thorns. [...] I'm just so lucky i got out when i did. [...] Anyways I came home, My brother let me in the back door and helped me take care of my wounds. Now i'm going to sleep. Night.

- Amy[...]

July 11th '07

Hey there,

So I'm sitting on my flight from Charlotte to Boston right now. [...] i went to St. Louis for my accepted students day. It wasn't too bad except I thought i'd meet quite a few more people. Maybe i'm less outgoing than i used to [...] We stayed in the Reinert dorm overnight and after a day of speeches and ice breakers I went to a party off campus with my roommate and another girl from our floor. I didn't have very much fun, there were lots of gorgeous girls there and I didn't have any money for booze. So I went back to the dorms and fell asleep. Sunday was a bit better. I got home really late because of plane delays. Was supposed to go to Alden's house Sunday night but I was way too tired and I had to get ready for Quebec!

- Amy

July 15th/16th 07
Today is a

GREAT

DAY

I got back from Quebec and I think I'm over Lon.
    ♥ Amy

7/17

Lon cheated on me. We just got off the phone and i cried. He told me after about an hour of me prying him about being honest with me. I don't want to get into details but [...] about a week before we broke up [...] i guess one thing led to another [...] I'm not too surprised, But I can't pretend i'm not hurt. [...] Especially after all the B/S he fed me about being honest with him. Throughout our relationship i suspected him of a lot but i always gave him the benefit of the doubt and I believed him when he promised he'd been faithful. It's one of the worst feelings ever to have one of your deepest suspicions confirmed. [...] He claims he didn't tell me because he felt 'soo guilty' and 'didn't want to hurt me or our friendship.' But after all the lies he's told me what am I supposed to believe? I've always thought omniscience would be such a wonderful thing but now i'm starting to wonder if it could also be a curse. Maybe ignorance truly is bliss.

    Good night.
        - Amy

Here begins another gap in Amy's journals. She did well during her first year at St. Louis University but decided she wanted to transfer to Boston College to be closer to home. But how much was to be closer to her new boyfriend, Oliver, whom she started seeing after a party in late 2007? Her initial application to transfer in the fall of 2008 was rejected. She tried again for spring 2009 with the essay that follows.

BC Transfer Essay 11-6-08[2]

In the fifteen months since I started college I have learned more about myself than I did through my entire high school career. In this new state of self-awareness, I have begun to realize the changes I must make so that I can achieve what I truly want out of my remaining years in college. While I have grown immeasurably from experiences at my current school, Saint Louis University (SLU), I have concluded that my personal goals and needs would be better fulfilled elsewhere.

One of the greatest transformations since becoming a college student is my attitude toward academics. I've abandoned the laid back, procrastinating approach I previously took toward my schoolwork to embrace my new-found desire for knowledge. The academic success I have achieved thus far reflects my efforts to learn as much as possible while I still have the resources to do so. Unfortunately, as academic achievement has become increasingly important to me, I have noticed the large percentage of my SLU peers to whom school is nothing but an obstacle that they look to overcome by the quickest and most simple means. This lack of academic enthusiasm, characteristic of many of my peers, has become a growing–and increasingly gnawing–issue for me as the school year has progressed, and I've realized that my intellectual interests would be better fostered at a more academically rigorous institution. Although my teachers and parents kept telling me that through the years, it has [taken] me until now to actually believe it myself.

While going through my initial college search process during high school, I was convinced that the only way to prove my independence involved creating a large geographical distance between my new school and my home. Moving half way across the country certainly increased my independence and responsibilities, however, I have since developed a longing to live in Massachusetts again and explore areas I failed to appreciate while living at home. While I've made a point to discover much of St. Louis, I've come to realize details about Boston that I previously took for granted, such as the

2. Amy is almost 20.

higher quality public transportation system (yes, the MBTA), the cultural diversity and the urban development–not to mention the scope of the medical resources for clinical education. Seeing the intellectual growth in several of my friends who chose to stay local for college has sparked my realization that personal effort, regardless of one's distance from home, is the key to gaining independence. I have decided that I want nothing more than to spend the remainder of my college years in the city I once tried to leave behind, only now with a greater appreciation for all that Boston has to offer.

My first three semesters at SLU have introduced me to the Jesuit mission, an aspect of the school I have come to love. The Jesuit mission promotes education of the whole, encouraging students to achieve success in every part of their lives. I feel that, while some institutions overemphasize the importance of the future and finding a job, SLU focuses more on helping its students grow into well-rounded, mature individuals. SLU also promotes the Jesuit tradition of service to others by offering thousands of service opportunities for students each year. My personal dedication to community service, which developed as a result of several volunteer service projects in high school, meshes perfectly with the Jesuit mission to serve, and I enjoy being part of a community that shares my enthusiasm in helping others. As the Jesuit influence has unexpectedly become an important part of my life over the past fifteen months, I've decided that I would like to continue my education at an institution that upholds similar values.

My decision to apply to Boston College once again, after being waitlisted as a transfer applicant for the fall semester, comes as a surprise to many of the people I encounter. I, however, do not see my experience last year as deterrence but rather as encouragement to now work even harder at proving my eligibility for admission into BC's competitive nursing program. As my academic and extracurricular achievements continue to grow in number, I hope that my hard work in college will soon overshadow my less than perfect high school record, thus representing the great personal changes I've accomplished during this period of time. I look forward to embracing each and every challenge that a BC environment would provide for me, and experiencing the benefits of an academic community I could once never have dreamed of joining.

Looking back at the past year, I am shocked by the progress I have made since my initial college application process. I realize that the self-knowledge I now hold was the missing element in my original college decision. As a matured woman with a much stronger sense of identity, and belief in my capabilities and aspirations, I have approached my third (and, hopefully, final) college search process knowing exactly what I do and do not want. Throughout the next three years I want to be pushed to be the absolute best I can in all aspects of life. The several reasons I would like to transfer back home stretch beyond the various factors I am able to objectively identify. I do not know if it's the excitement I experience whenever I see a Red Sox hat, or the strangeness I feel around non-Bostonians who actually pronounce their R's, but I have realized that for the remainder of my college years I belong nowhere else than "down by river" at Boston College.

....

Amy was admitted to the nursing school at Boston College for the second semester of sophomore year, but we have not found journals from her college years. Before returning to Boston, she was prescribed the medication Suboxone by a psychiatrist in St. Louis in March 2008, spring of her first year. She later told us that it was to help her deal with cravings, but not that it is prescribed for people suffering from addiction to prescription opioid painkillers or heroin.

Amy started at Boston College in January 2009. She loved her courses. As far as we know, she didn't use opiates during her first semester. That summer she worked as a personal care assistant for an elderly woman, took a three-week intensive microbiology class, and started using opiates again. At some point she began seeing a drug counselor at Boston College, Mr. Goodruco. The following passage describes her attempt to self-detox in August 2009.

8/22[3] Sick sick sick sick sick sick sick.. that's what I am. Plane to Hawaii-6hrs of dope [[heroin]] sickness.

8/26 That was just about one of the worst time periods of my life. I didn't think the sickness would come so full force but I guess considering the amount of heroin I was shooting (at least a 70 bag at least 5 days a week for at least a few weeks before Hawaii), going down to nothing would torture my body into multi-symptoms of confusion and withdrawal. It started in about 2 hours into my flight from Pheonix to Hawaii and I think I may have taken a Suboxone too soon because in about 20 minutes my body turned from feeling slightly off to full fledged kicks, cold flashes and desperation. Looking back, I never want to go through that ever ever ever again, but I am so scared that I'll return to Boston and get right back into dope.

---

3. Amy is 20½.

Even today, Wednesday, my cravings are extremely heavy.

Day 1 (Saturday 8/22)- no fun, I'm done.

Day 2- feelin (sic) like poo and a little blue, don't know what to do

Day 3- WHY ME???

Day 4- still craving more

Day 5 (today, Wednesday)- will I get through this alive?

Reasons to stay clean:
-Money in my bank account
-Salvage things with Oliver
-Make my family proud instead of tolerant of me
-Give Mr. Goodruco some faith in me
-Have normal relationships with my roommates and others at BC
-Won't need to miss fall semester for rehab

During the fall of 2009, Amy started her nursing clinicals, meaning she was learning to take care of patients in the hospital. But her nursing instructors noticed that something wasn't right. And so did I. She started talking with me about wanting to come off the Suboxone, which might mean going to rehab. She wanted to break up with her boyfriend, Oliver. One October afternoon I also found a needle in her laundry. And many of her stories didn't make sense. I'll never forget the Saturday she was eating a tuna sub for lunch at home and started nodding off, which can be a sign of opiate use.

**AMELIA
CARUSO**
STUDENT NURSE

Finally, Amy told me that she wanted me to meet with her and Mr. Goodruco. On November 16th in that meeting, Amy admitted that she was addicted to heroin and wanted to take a medical leave of absence to go to treatment. She wrote the following email a few hours later.

11/16/2009 9:17 p.m.

From: Amelia Caruso

Subject: books

Hi Mom and Dad,

At my last appointment, Dr. [Pedreia] recommended a book pair, "Beautiful Boy" and "Tweak." One is written by a father (David Sheff) and the other by his son (Nic Sheff), who struggled with a meth addiction. Anyways, she and I think reading these books might help us understand each others perspectives and behaviors a bit [...]

Thanks again for all your support and understanding through this process. I know the last 24 hours have been extremely tough on the whole family and I'm so overwhelmed with guilt :(It hurts me sooo bad to see the disappointed looks in your eyes and to see you crying, but I'm just glad the lies are over and everything is out in the open now. I think this process might really change my relationship with you guys, for the better. I promise to put everything I have towards my recovery and I'm really looking forward to going on this journey.

Love always,
Amy

Amy wrote the following notes shortly before she entered treatment. "Stress and Behavior" is a psychology class she was taking during the fall semester.

Onset: I continued my prescription for about a week until there were no more pills, but when the prescription had run out I felt an abnormal emptiness that I had never previously encountered. Later that year, after suffering injuries from a ski accident, I was prescribed a month long supply of Oxycodone and this time when I stopped using my prescription these empty feelings were accompanied by a slew of flu like symptoms which I would later recognize as withdrawal.

Progression: Before my two medical interventions I had never been the type to experiment with drugs or alcohol, but the harsh contrast from constant exposure to a strong narcotic to nothing at all propelled me to actively seek out more, and before I knew it my opiate problem had escalated to the point where I was using almost every day.

Now, in writing this essay I am of course concerned about the implications of admitting my slip into such a lowly esteemed sector of society, that of the drug addict, but as I stress about the opinions of those who read this, I also realize the importance of expressing this difficult part of my journey and, in a way, lifting it from my chest.

As I learned in Stress and Behavior, having one or two "soft addictions" can be healthy but by summer my opiate addiction was the opposite of soft and would soon alter my life in drastic ways.

I feel that details regarding the extent of my addiction are trivial compared to the stresses that resulted, so for the purpose of this essay I will merely state that my addiction was out of control. It pains me just to recall the [disrespect] for my absent values, constant lying and neglect of relationships to name only a few. I did both to sustain and protect my drug use. Every day seemed a new obstacle as I struggled to find sources of money, and met with some of the sickest people I have ever met, and face the painful physically torturous pains of withdrawal, all the while trying to live a superficially "normal" life, concealing my habit from those closest to me.

Many people who have not themselves experienced drug addiction wonder why addicts [weren't] able to "just quit." Believe it or not, this was a question that constantly haunted me as I dealt with the shame and embarrassment of not being able to control my own actions and probably one of the factors preventing me from coming forth with my problem and asking for help. One common perception is that drug abuse depends on individual choice and any desperate person who allowed themselves to fall into such a circumstance would be considered weak and unambitious, the scum of society for not successfully climbing out.

....

On Saturday, November 21st, we drove Amy to a treatment facility ninety minutes from home. She would spend her first six days in the Triangle detox unit, then transfer to the Rhombus rehab facility. Her treatment would conclude at the Circle Center, a program where women in recovery lived together.

Nine
Rehab Journals[1]

11/25

Today is my 5th day at Triangle Treatment center. After over 6 months of progressive and tumultuous drug use I finally decided I'd been fucking up long enough and, ~~and~~ with the help of Mr. Goodruco, told my mother about my addiction and the fact that I would ~~not~~ be taking the remainder of the semester off. Worst meeting of my entire life — ~~my~~ my mother's initial anger followed by panic, ~~grief~~, disappointment...

The entire week I was so excited to get sober but, then again, I had the drug in my system ~~a~~ at the present time, not realizing the difficult work I would soon face...

I've had several great discussions with people here and a few have asked me whether or not I'm ~~serious about~~ serious about getting sober. They ask, how bad do I "want it"? I'm on day 4 of protocol (aka suboxone administration) and I must say that at times, my cravings are unbearable. Some people here talked about not being "done" with ~~ap~~ their drug of choice (especially in the case of opiates), and I wonder if I'm one of those patients. I wonder if the whole reason I'm doing the 30 day program isn't to lower my tolerance or gain my mothers trust back. That's my "disease" talking.

---

1. Amy is nearly 21.

I know how much I want and need my sober life back. I know the real Amy is inside me somewhere and I need to get her back before my life turns to complete shit. But am I willing to do the work? I'm one lazy son of a bitch and I'm going to need constant reminder of my misery in order to heal.

—Until Later—

Oliver is... ahhhhhh! I ended up staying at Triangle until Friday morning and was able to sneak my cell into Rhombus. Now he's like going crazy because I'm not calling him very often and thinks I don't care and questions whether or not I love him. I don't really think I do, I mean...

11/29/09

Dear Mom, Dad

Thanks so much for coming to visit me today. I'm still feeling sort of crappy and the "comfort medications" only make me tired, so I apologize for not being more upbeat. Things should be much better by the next time I see you all. I hope everything is going okay back home — it hurts me to see the disappointment and sadness in your eyes. I just want you to know that I'm constantly missing and thinking of you but, more importantly, I'm doing a lot of introspection, and taking in all that Triangle has to offer. I feel like I'm already at a much better place (mentally) than I was and, although I have much more work to do, I have a positive outlook regarding the future. I could not have asked for a more supportive family and I truly, from the bottom of my heart, appreciate all that you continue to do for me. I am in the right hands — these guys seem to know what they're talking about! So just keep sending your prayers and blessings and I'll continue doing the work I need to be doing here. I love you all so so much and I am incredibly grateful for your love + effort. Please don't hesitate to bring anything up with me if you want to talk!

I love you all *very much!*

♡ Amy

Rhombus Rehab   Day 5 ⇒ Days clean: 11

I don't know what I want. All I know is that I'm
sick of acting like a hypocrit and leading a double life.
I have this boyfriend who I tell I love just about
every 5 minutes but I tell all my friends and family
that I don't want anything to do with him. Truthfully,
I know that it's just about over between Oliver and
I — he just doesn't stimulate me intellectually,
emotionally, sexually... I mean a year and a half of
faking it?   How much can I take, really? Haha,
but on a more serious note, I'm scared shitless of
being alone and without somebody to talk to every
time I'm happy, sad, desperate, crazy... I'm terrified of
facing the world without him by my side. That,
however, gives me all the more reason to break up with
him after the separation that rehab will provide. Now that
I'm sober, I see absolutely no value in being with him.
I now understand why he didn't push me to go
to treatment — why he even helped me get drugs when
he knew how addicted I was — heroin was the shield
over my eyes — the glue that kept Oliver and I
together for 6 months longer than I ever should
have been with him. And worst of all, I've spent
the last year and a half focusing all my

AC ♥ ?

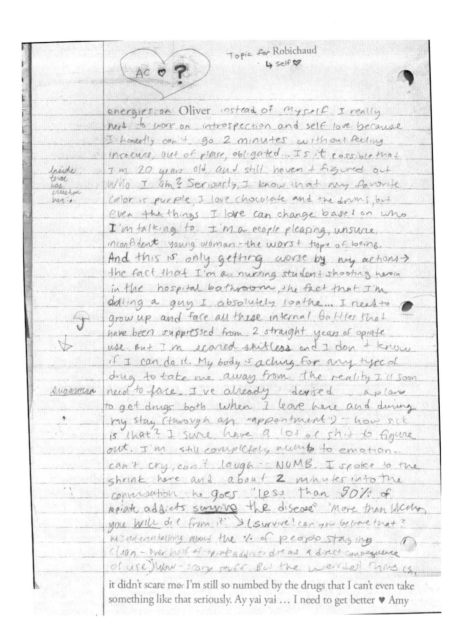

Topic for Robichaud
↳ self ♥

energies on Oliver instead of myself. I really
need to work on introspection and self love because
I honestly can't go 2 minutes without feeling
insecure, out of place, obligated... Is it possible that
I'm 20 years old and still haven't figured out
who I am? Seriously, I know that my favorite
color is purple, I love chocolate and the drums, but
even the things I love can change based on who
I'm talking to. I'm a people pleasing, unsure,
inconfident young woman - the worst type of being.
And this is only getting worse by my actions →
the fact that I'm a nursing student shooting heroin
in the hospital bathroom, the fact that I'm
dating a guy I absolutely loathe... I need to
grow up and face all these internal battles that
have been suppressed from 2 straight years of opiate
use. But I'm scared shitless and I don't know
if I can do it. My body is aching for any type of
drug to take me away from the reality I'll soon
need to face. I've already devised a plan
to get drugs both when I leave here and during
my stay (through an "appointment") - how sick
is that? I sure have a lot of shit to figure
out. I'm still completely numb to emotion -
can't cry, can't laugh - NUMB. I spoke to the
shrink here and about 2 minutes into the
conversation he goes "Less than 50% of
opiate addicts surviving the disease" "More than likely
you will die from it" → (survive! can you believe that?
he's not even talking about the % of people staying
clean - over half of opiate addicts die as a direct consequence
of use) Wow - scary stuff. But the weirdest thing is,
it didn't scare me. I'm still so numbed by the drugs that I can't even take
something like that seriously. Ay yai yai … I need to get better ♥ Amy

Inside that was crushin her.

Sugarman

12/3/09

Day 6 off Suboxone completed. Starting to feel better. One significant thing today—I was moved from the room I was staying in (a double with a private bathroom) because according to the staff, Marta and I "need some space." I don't know what that's all about because me and her weren't even that close. I mean, we talked about our relationships and other stuff and got along just fine. My initial reaction was that Marta asked for me to be moved and that thought is still prying at the back of my mind—she didn't react very strongly when I mentioned the room change in women's group and even went as far as to say "oh well I have fun by myself anyways." Then she's just been M. I. A. all night. It's so hard to read this girl, but why am I focusing my energies on her anyways? Maybe this move is for the best....I can't tell if it's my self esteem beating me down or if Marta is just acting weird. I have a feeling both our low self-esteems contribute to the awkwardness between us (ever since I figured out she likes girls I haven't been able to strike up conversation or even look in her direction w/out feeling awkward). I think it's fear of rejection and wondering about each other's opinions that's caused the slow, nervous beginnings. Agh I'm so confused tho b/c we had such a good conversation the other night for like 4 hours.

Wow...see, this is why it might be a good idea to separate us. I obv. care too much about being liked and not enough about my sobriety...more on her later...I'm just terrified b/c this girl Claire I met at detox comes to Rhombus tomorrow and I'm scared those 2 will branch out leaving me alone. Oh well, I need to let go of these anxieties and just let fate handle it. AAGH. Feeling emotionally absent—numb. I don't know if this is because of the heroin, the withdrawals, or maybe the fact that I haven't been focusing? Or Maybe I've just forgotten how to experience feelings. Either way, I'm at a total emotionall plateau. _____ (the only ____ dude here) told me to look at it as a "balance" instead of numbness, and to appreciate my mood swing absence. It's all about how you look at it ...

Till later,
Amy

12-7-09

Out of Marta's room into a single, then moved back into the room w/ this girl Claire (not the girl I thought but wicked sweet). Lots of thoughts still revolve around a certain someone here. She was asking Oliver why I switched too! Mixed signals. HIV and Hep C tests came back negative! _____ got Hep tho ☹

Hepatitis C is a contagious disease that can last a lifetime and lead to serious liver problems. Most people become infected with the Hepatitis C virus by sharing needles to inject drugs.

Night,
Amy

Amy wrote her SLU friend Patrick a letter on December 7th, in which she asked forgiveness for neglecting their friendship during her autumn relapse, and to pray that she would stay clean and be able to visit for spring break. She included the haunting sentence, "Remember, life is too short (I realize that now more than ever)..."

"But though they may be parted, there is still a chance that they will see ... there will be an answer, Let It Be"

—The Beatles

12-8-09

I feel like the drugs have taken over my soul. What happened to the strong, motivated young woman I was last spring? The impending doom sets in as I realize my disease has never been this bad. Thinking back to the near end of my "sober" 10-½ months, I remember fiening for a fix to change pace from the Suboxone monotony, but because I was nearly finished with school for the year I told myself to wait. I can't help but think that this run up was planned and expected, but I have no idea when I planned to stop. Maybe before fall semester? Maybe never ... Drugs have been my plan, my sole coping skills, for 6 years now. At the beginning of this last run I still had my head on straight. I had the aftertaste of sobriety reminding me that I didn't need to live the way I was. I truly thought I would only use for a short period, then get back to my normal life. But as the use increased, my control quickly diminished, and, once into the "chronic" stage of my addiction, I lost sight of what was most important to me. I stand today as heroin's puppet, feeling as if every fiber in my being is dull, responding only to the stimulation of potential drug use. The disease has a stronghold—a white-knuckled fist, fingernails, ripping through my skin, prying deeper and deeper into my body. I wonder what I can possibly do to break free from it's grasp and remember the life I used to love and show up for.

17 days clean today. Seventeen! Crazy because I know if I was out there I would have gotten high just about every day. Starting to get scared about leaving here—what I'm going to do, what my life will be like. My fear isn't big enough though. I'm scared my disease won't let me go....

12-9

Just finished Day 17 and am sitting in bed at 12:45 am on Dec 9th. Got another 23h 15 min to go. ONE DAY AT A TIME! Talking to Oliver less and plan to break up with him on Thursday. I'm terrified, but have never felt more ready

"Though they may be parted, there is still a chance that they will see, there will be an answer, Let it Be"

I need to do this now, while I still have the support of the wonderful people here. If I leave here, 1 of 3 things will happen:

1. I'll relapse instantly and stay w/ him
2. I'll dump him and then relapse to deal w/ the stress
3. I'll stay clean but be too weak to dump him

Most likely, I'd take option #1 real fast. So I realized the need to break things off while I'm still here, but I don't think he has any idea. The family counselor is going to come help me do it when Oliver comes here on Thursday. I have plans for him to sneak something in but he doesn't know it yet and I don't think it would be the best idea. Although, I could probably do that and have "just 1." OMGosh, please Lord save me from the grips of this disease. I keep telling myself how much things will change once I'm without Oliver. I hope it's true...
Amy

12-9-09

Woke up to snow and a beautiful view from the backyard. It's so gorgeous outside, and the weather is one of a million things I should appreciate today. I know I need to change my attitude but have no idea how to do it. It's sort of hard when every neuron in my brain in some way magnets to the idea of heroin.

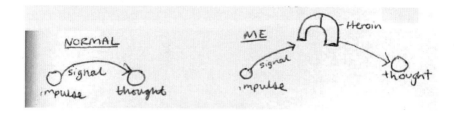

I can't even get an ounce of information through my head without an interruption from the Heroin PSA [[Public Service Announcement]] – Am I f---ed? I can't help but think YES. I feel like everyone who has successfully quit dope has used the disgusting, desperate low of their "rock bottom" to mirror in their recovery – to not only motivate their sobriety, but to have a very high standard for which to reflect the quality of my recovery work.

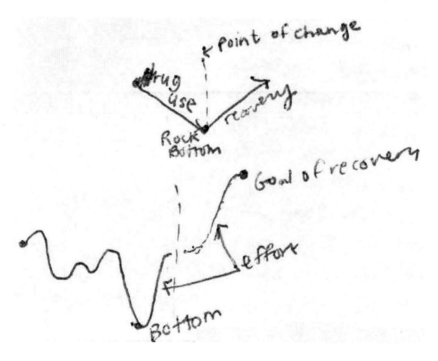

So in my mind I'm well aware of where my drug use will lead → the effect on my body and soul, the consequences on my family and my life and my future. I've been told exactly what will happen if I go out again. But just like they say, you can't scare an addict. I think there's a reason the professionals say hitting a bottom is necessary—I can imagine the dangers and the consequences all day long but if I've never lived it, if my brain can't feel or actually place me in that cardboard box on the side of the road eating out of a trash bag, then how the f--- is that supposed to scare me out of using?

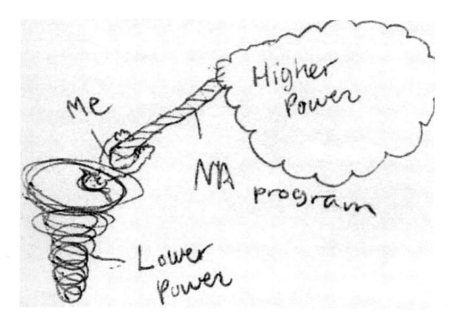

I feel like at my lowest point, I had lost money, trust, friends and school, and put just about everything on the line (I would have lost them had I been out there, right now). But I didn't actually lose some things. I always had a place to live, a meal, a lover, the support of my parents. As I look into the rear-view mirror of my life, I see the destruction, but I also see a liveable life. If I could hang out doing dope every day while still doing my thing and semi-handling sh--, then what motivation have I to live the same life without my beloved heroin, feeling all the pain and struggles of everyday life? So I know these obvious, straightforward concepts, but I can't get them all the way through my brain, through the barbed wire fence my addiction has built.

In the group I'm in right now, the counselor spoke about a girl on methadone maintenance who claimed "this sobriety thing isn't all it's cracked up to be." I'm having a hard time w/ this as well. It's like because I'm sober, everybody (including myself) expected me to suddenly wake up and "see the light." But I'm still navigating my way out of my tunnel. I just experienced a revelation regarding my progress and sobriety. So, the first step claims that your life has become unmanageable as a result of your addiction. I think I'm having a lot of trouble with this step, possibly regarding the higher nature of my bottom, but more because of the success I seemed to have with the Suboxone maintenance. For a year and a half I was able to live a normal, manageable life while every day taking an opiate. My body is used to feeding its most extreme desire all day every day, while still going to school, keeping up relationships, having money, and everything else. Though I was in no way _LIVING_ the life I could be, I was "successfully" keeping up a habit for a long period of time. Now my disease is trying to trick me into thinking I can do the same with heroin. Until I let go of this and accept the inevitable undebatable truth, I'll _never_ get clean. In order to beat this disease I need to do one crucial thing: outsmart myself.

....

By the "First Step," Amy is referring to the program of Narcotics Anonymous, a so-called 12-step group to support those in recovery from narcotics addiction.

A common concept in recovery is that until a person hits a "rock bottom" they won't be ready to pursue recovery from their disease. Amy worried that because she was still functioning in many ways, her "bottom" wasn't quite a "rock bottom."

12-9-09 = My official sober date from Oliver. It's now a little past midnight and I'm still feeling the high from breaking things off. I don't know if it's because of the withdrawals or because I was just so ready, but for some reason I don't feel upset or scared by this breakup. I'm so free and no longer a possession of Oliver's. He was bawling, sobbing, begging. I felt nothing ...I feel as if ... I lost my train of thought. PROUD OF MYSELF. That took balls, kid.

12-?

Visited Circle Center w/ Marta. The place was nice, but I'm wary about being around 30 freakin women all the time. Marta isn't too thrilled to be going on Monday. As the breakup and the lack of drugs become more of a reality, I realize how freaking scared I am to face the world. I feel as if I can't talk to anyone and I'm out of place everywhere I go. When I'm out in society I feel like this evil, two sided bitch because of my secret heroin addiction. When I'm in rehab I feel like I don't fit in w/ the junkies because I was never selling my ass or getting arrested or living in the streets. I think what it comes down to is that I can't fully commit to one thing a) because I'm so interested/see the benefits in many things and b) I'm scared I'll never be good enough if I put all my effort into 1 thing.

12-15-09

<u>RESERVATIONS</u>

• Losing my connect and, therefore, getting strong urges to use

• Drinking w/ my college friends and the "party life"—esp. on my 21st bday

• I'll miss the RUSH and warm tingly "everything is okay" feeling

• Blunt rides w/ the homies

• The heroin weight loss program

• I'm young and might 'have another run in me'
• Needle addiction—fear of relapse and using a dirty needle—so why not keep some of my own around just in case?

12-20-09

It's snowing! Beautiful, wisping, white, fluffy snow. Chilling in my Room w/ my amazing roomie Claire. Good meeting tonight—I saw ___ w/ his [new hairdo] and sense of humor, ____, ____ (his glf can't have an abortion b/c she's [further along than] they thought), ____ (this sweet girl who has really reached out to me)… ____ and ____ got their 30 day keychains! My feelings about sobriety and overall morale boost when I'm around people at NA and AA that I can talk to, even for just a minute. I need to make sure socializing and people don't make up my recovery, or become new addictions.

DON'T JUST KNOW. APPLY.
— Amy

....

A common practice at both Alcoholics Anonymous (AA) and Narcotics Anonymous (NA) is that a person earns a keychain or a coin for achieving a certain number of days of not using alcohol or drugs. Keychains and coins are given at 30, 60, and 90 days; 6 months; and annual anniversaries.

Last Journal Entry

12-21-09

Moved to the "Circle Center" today with my roomie Claire. Lots of cool people here, but I was getting so anxious and depressed worrying about making friends.

I'm starting to realize just how sick I am. I read a pamphlet about self-acceptance from NA that read "Because we could not accept ourselves, we expected to be rejected by others. We would not allow anyone to get close to us for fear that if they really knew us, they would also hate us".

I'm terrified of rejection because I despise myself so much. My whole life I've been trying to be or act like someone else, anyone else. Why can't I just be?

My disease is controlling 90% of the thoughts that are going through my head. It tells me that I shouldn't be here. I won't fit in. Everyone hates me. I'll never beat the cravings.

It tells me that I can't recover without reaching a rock bottom. That jail might be the turning point that sets me straight. It has me scheming about ways to make money like selling my body, dating my drug dealer, stripping, robbing houses, selling back my textbooks and other belongings. It tells me I have a whole new world of drug addiction to experience before I can really make an effort to get clean. It assures me that relapses are part of recovery.

My disease pounds self loathing and insecurity into my mind. It perpetually reminds me

that I have a big nose, I'm getting fat, I'm
awkward and weird, I'm never going to make it in
the world.

Worst of all, it tries to convince me that I don't
have a disease but am simply going through a
phase. It tells me that anyone who tries heroin
will become addicted, so how can I be singledout
as one of these addicts. It tells me I managed to
handle all my drug use before, so why can't it work
with heroin?

COME ON AMY, JUST INDULGE AND PICK
UP ONE MORE TIME.

NO! I've noticed my thoughts are very negative
lately. I've been fantasizing about overdosing
for a quick, painless death and telling myself
I'd be doing everyone a favor (including
myself).

I'm sick.
I'm weak.

Need Help.

But do I really want it?

—Amy (and her disease)

Epilogue

Amy convinced her counselor at Circle Center to issue her a twelve-hour pass for Christmas day. Her dad and I picked her up in the morning, and our family had brunch with relatives. We came home and opened presents, and she gave us the card below.

My dearest family,

This Christmas season has been unlike past holidays and unfortunately this means I wasn't able to acquire gifts for you. I wish the circumstances were different but, as you all know, I'm working hard to improve the most important thing of all: my

Warm Christmas Wishes

health. Though I have nothing material to give, I can promise to bring my love, my gratitude and (of course) my sobriety. I look forward to the time I'll be spending with you over Christmas and will surely treasure each moment we share as a family.

Thanks for all your love and support throughout these last few months. It's meant the world to me.

I LOVE YOU ALL SO MUCH!

XOXO
Amy.

At 2:11 p.m. she posted on Facebook: *home for the day ~ SO grateful and blessed to be with my loved ones! merry Christmas:)*

One condition of Amy's pass was that she attend a twelve-step meeting. I dropped her off at 3:00 and picked her up promptly at 4:30. Back home, she paid some bills online and made a list of the seven people to whom I would give the boxes of chocolates that she had ordered. Our family ate dinner at an Indian restaurant. To this day, I regret that we didn't take a group photo.

After dinner I hugged her good-bye and said "I love you, be safe." Her brother drove her back to Circle Center, stopping first at her apartment.

The next day, as Amy's dad, her sister, and I were driving to visit my parents, we received a phone call at 4:36 p.m. It was our son, who had been called by the Circle Center staff. Amy had been found unconscious and transported to the hospital.

We turned around and drove toward the hospital, but we were hours away. At 8:16 we called our son, who had arrived at the hospital with his girlfriend. He told us that Amy could not make it. The emergency team had worked on her for almost two hours and could not bring her back.

We'll never know the source of the fatal drugs, though some people suspect she obtained them during the time she was supposed to be at the twelve-step meeting. The toxicology report cited heroin and cocaine—a "speedball." We'll also never know whether Amy intended to overdose, a possibility she mentioned in her final journal entry.

We buried her on New Year's Eve, weeks shy of her 21st birthday.

I really miss my daughter. I feel cheated because I was counting on having her around into my old age. After Amy died, I found a post-it note on which she'd scribbled "sometimes i want to apologize to the girl i was 10 years ago ... for not becoming the girl she dreamed of being 10 years from then."

Resources

Amy's story shows that her addiction had roots in underlying issues including anxiety, depression, and low self esteem. While her journals did not point to any childhood trauma, perhaps the pregnancy scare was more traumatic than anyone realized at the time. And while it did not appear that she was bullied, Amy's words perhaps say it best, "If high school's supposed to be the best years of my life then what the fuck is the rest of my life gunna be like???"

Unfortunately, our society still lacks enough of the right resources for people with mental health issues and substance use disorders and addiction. Help can be found, but it often takes a lot of effort to find the right fit, especially for young people. Resources are constantly evolving, so instead of trying to provide a list here that may soon be obsolete, it's best to start in your community—maybe even in your own home (remember when Amy said "I thought she'd be angry but she was actually very supportive. I told her I was scared…")

In a life-threatening emergency, call 911. For non-emergencies, places to start include supportive relatives, family friends, school guidance counselors, pediatricians or a local health clinic. Support groups can be an outstanding source of referrals, keeping in mind that every person's situation is different and it's all about the right fit, diagnosis, and treatment plan. Local, state and national hotlines can also point you to resources.

If you or a loved one needs help, please remember that one of Amy's friends said, "it's not snitching, it's about saving lives." Or as one principal says, "it's not about getting someone in trouble, it's about getting them the help they need." And as one of my former students, now a nurse, says, "If I had known then what I know now, I wish I would have **not** kept silent."

Acknowledgements

The ultimate thanks go to Amy for the gift of her journals. The spark for the book came from Lily's mom, with critical early affirmation from my dear friend and colleague Marianne Pugatch LICSW.

I am grateful to Debbie and Carol, who helped me proofread the transcriptions. The decision to keep going was affirmed when my husband Jeff Caruso, friend Ali M., school librarian Kathy A., and Dr. Emeric Bojarski read the raw transcription and were sounding boards and sanity-checkers. Shannon Barefield at The Editorial Department, brought her expertise as a Young Adult editor to shape the story and improve readability without sacrificing authenticity.

The edited manuscript was carefully commented upon by Audrey, Mary G., Lily's mom, Christina N (soon to be a Licensed Mental Health Counselor), Shannon Mountain-Ray LICSW, Erica W., Barb W., and Anne M. Your thoughtful feedback has helped keep the book true to Amy's spirit and reassured me that this work is appropriate for its intended readers.

Finally, there was no question about who I wanted to design this book: Laurel Lloyd's brilliant ideas have produced a work that surpassed even what she accomplished with *Heroin's Puppet*.

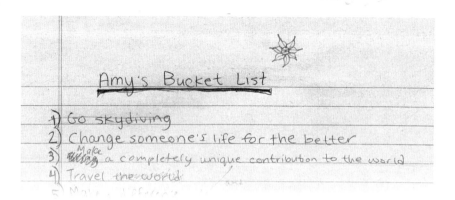

1) ~~Go skydivingpage~~

2) Change someone's life for the better

3) ~~Bring~~ Make a completely unique contribution to the world

4) Travel ~~the world~~

5) Make a difference

6) Touch someone's heart

7) Run a marathon

8) Find my spiritual awakening

9) Learn to play all sorts of instruments

10) Finish college and fulfill my potential

11) Try something new every day

12) Reconnect w/ friends + family and have meaningful relationships

13) See the sunrise from every state

14) Become and stay sober

15) Find pleasure in the simple things => The pleasure of what we ~~enjoy is lost by wanting more~~